Strong, Sweet and Dry

Strong, Sweet & Dry

A GUIDE TO VERMOUTH, PORT, SHERRY, MADEIRA AND MARSALA

Becky Sue Epstein

REAKTION BOOKS

Published by Reaktion Books Ltd
Unit 32, Waterside
44–48 Wharf Road
London N1 7UX, UK
www.reaktionbooks.co.uk

First published 2020

Printed and bound in Malta by Gutenberg Press Ltd

A catalogue record for this book is available from the British Library

ISBN 978 1 78914 152 8

Contents

—◆—

N

Porto

Port

SPAIN

Lisbon

PORTUGAL

Sherry

Jerez

*Atlantic
Ocean*

Madeira

MOROCCO

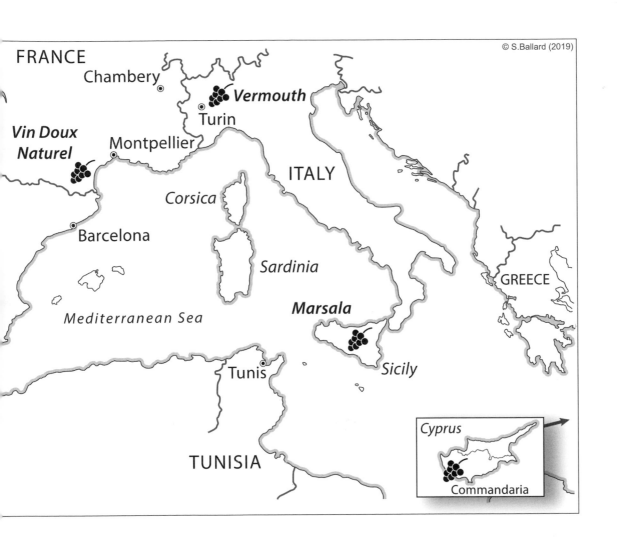

FRANCE

Chambery ⊙

Vermouth

Turin ⊙

Vin Doux Naturel

Montpellier ⊙

ITALY

Corsica

Barcelona ⊙

Sardinia

Marsala

GREECE

Mediterranean Sea

Tunis ⊙

Sicily

TUNISIA

© S.Ballard (2019)

Cyprus

Commandaria

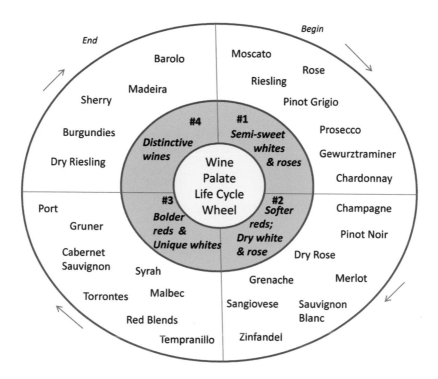

Wine Palate Life Cycle Wheel

Begin

Moscato
Rose
Riesling
Pinot Grigio
Prosecco
Gewurztraminer
Chardonnay

#1 *Semi-sweet whites & roses*

Champagne
Pinot Noir
Dry Rose
Grenache
Merlot
Sangiovese
Sauvignon Blanc
Zinfandel

#2 *Softer reds; Dry white & rose*

Tempranillo
Red Blends
Torrontes
Malbec
Syrah
Cabernet Sauvignon
Gruner
Port

#3 *Bolder reds & Unique whites*

End

Barolo
Madeira
Sherry
Burgundies
Dry Riesling

#4 *Distinctive wines*

We appreciate fortified wines more and more as our palates mature, according to recent groundbreaking research by Dr Liz Thach at Sonoma State University in California.

Introduction

—◆—

Rich wines, generous wines, strong wines. Who wouldn't be drawn to wines with these charismatic names? High-spirited wines that have been relished for centuries, in a variety of countries: these are fortified wines. According to the latest research, the appreciation of fortified wines represents the ultimate evolution of the wine-drinker's palate.

Vermouth, port, sherry, Madeira, Marsala, vin doux naturel. The six major wines discussed in this book have been chosen for their enjoyability as well as their significance in the narrative of wine history. They are all European in origin, made with traditional wine grapes fermented into wine, then fortified and aged. 'Fortified' simply means that pure spirit (usually a clear, unaged grape brandy) is added to the wine while it ferments, stopping the fermentation at a particular time. The result is wine with an alcohol level that is a little higher than table wine, which is appealing not only in taste, but in the wines' ability to age for decades, even centuries.

Fortified wines display enticing flavours and fragrances. They possess multifaceted histories that connect science, discovery, trade and commerce in the modern world. Today, fortified wines stand at the intriguing intersection of wine, spirits and cocktails. Everywhere, there are new cocktails being fashioned with rare and wonderful spices, liqueurs, spirits and wines – including fortified wines. In this lusty re-flowering of mixed drinks, it's as if fortified wines have woken up from a long, arid winter. Suddenly, the dry leaves have been cleared away; bright streams have appeared and have instantly been gathered for consumption – in cocktails, as aperitif wines and even for dessert. But where did they come from?

This book tells the stories of the world's most significant forti-fied wines from their early histories, through centuries of conflicts, tempests and victories, to the present day. The fortified wines discussed here have been fashioned with care by winemakers fol-lowing paths of excellence that have been demonstrated by many generations of wine producers. They are all made from traditional wine grapes (*Vitis vinifera*) that have been fermented into wine, then fortified and aged. After a season of growth in the vineyard, harvest and vinification, the wines have been fortified with pure grape spirit at precise moments in their development.

Ultimately, fortified wines are the enthralling result of months and years of evolving to perfection in barrels and in bottles, some in bright sunlight, others in cool, airy wine warehouses, still more in the sultry darkness of underground wine cellars. Many of these wines have experienced decades of extreme ageing, ultimately evolving with extra dimensionality in their aromas, flavours and finishes. Their renown has transcended centuries, and the wines themselves have been welcomed by discerning drinkers everywhere.

Fortified wines are now being imbibed by aficionados, collectors and generations of upscale restaurant and bar patrons looking for fresh thrills in their glasses. Mixologists and wine directors are joyously rediscovering fortified wines and employing their spicy aromas and lively flavours to create a new era for wine lovers as well as cocktail and spirit lovers.

Sherry has already proven its worth in cocktails, and other fortified wines have followed. Port is having a renaissance, with bartenders returning to using it as a cocktail base, just as they did in the nineteenth century, before rum, vodka and gin were popular.

Well-known cocktail consultant Michael Lazar clarifies the process of putting together cocktails:

> An immediate advantage of wine-based ingredients (such as vermouth and [other] fortified wines) is that they provide a measure of acidity that spirit-based ingredients can't. Plus they can also add elements found no place else: oxidative flavours that can really add depth to a drink. And finally, added in the form of dry/blanc vermouths or sercial madeira, they can help offset sugars coming from other ingredients without adding a lot of flavour on their own.

Vermouth is one of his favourite ingredients, Lazar says. 'It's the acidity in vermouths complemented by all the other flavours they provide, that makes them such welcome additions to spirit driven cocktails, or really any cocktail in which we use them.'

Eminent bar educator Andy Seymour explains, 'Cocktails get people to places they wouldn't normally get to – laughable in the 1990s but normal now.' Seymour uses one particular fortified wine as an illustration: 'There's a very traditional place for port and that should never go away. But don't be so reverential that we can't enjoy port in a different way: cocktails. [For example] a lot of bartenders are trying out Manhattan style cocktails with tawny port [as a base].'

In restaurants, for both wine directors and their customers, fortified wines are a new direction that entices explorers who are interested as much in novelty as they are in re-creating retro experiences.

Fortified wines have their greatest successes in food pairings when they are suggested by staff or on a menu. They are still a very small part of the total wine sales of any establishment, but they are growing every day, in the U.S., the UK and in forward-thinking bars and restaurants around the globe.

Simple and refreshing:
Cocchi Vermouth di Torino
poured over ice, garnished
with orange zest.

1
Vermouth

———◆———

Most people who drink cocktails have sampled vermouth, often without being aware of it, and usually without even knowing what vermouth is. Vermouth can be red or white, sweet or dry. Announcing itself with fragrances of spices and herbs, vermouth is known for its exotic and pleasing aromas, and its interplay of bitter and sweet components on the palate.

In fact this is the definition of vermouth: an aromatized, fortified wine. And this is what has galvanized the mixology world in recent years: the rediscovery of a wine that adds unusual dry or sweet elements to a cocktail, blending beautifully with a variety of spirits, bitters and citrus accents, making it easy to create perfect balance in a glass.

Vermouth Before Cocktails

Was vermouth created as a cocktail element? Absolutely not. In the eighteenth century, when vermouth became popular in Europe, there was no cocktail movement in existence. There was no tradition of blending finished wines and spirits. Lacking the modern transportation network we have today, Europeans in every region were limited to consuming their own locally produced drink. Sometimes it was simply wine from local vineyards, or it could be a *marc* or grappa-style beverage: a strong alcoholic drink made with fruit pomace (the remains after grapes have been pressed for wine). Sometimes it was a distilled spirit – a brandy made from grapes or whatever other fruit or grain grew locally.

Vermouth was a new development in the 1700s in Torino (the city now known to English-speakers as Turin), Italy. It was a wine that was fortified with alcohol and aromatized with many herbs and spices, but aimed at the general consumer, and not meant to be a medicinal treatment. Much as the 'cordials' of today were originally considered enjoyable versions of health tonics, vermouth in essence straddled the line. It was basically an aperitif, an appetite stimulant taken before the meal. This is a good rationalization for drinking vermouth, whether or not it is true.

Vermouth also became popular because people enjoyed its taste. It had a familiar flavour profile for inhabitants of this part of Piedmont (now in northern Italy), with native mountain herbs and a well-established combination of sweetness and bitterness. Sweetened, herbed wines had been in existence in Europe for centuries by the time vermouth came along. In Turin, exotic spices were also added to vermouth because this city was on a spice-trading corridor that led first from Asia to Genoa by ship, then over land through Turin to more northern European cities.

There are basically three traditional, international styles of vermouth: red, sweet white and dry white. Red is called *rosso* in Italian and *rouge* in French. It was the first style created, followed by sweet white, which is called *bianco* in Italian and *blanc* in French. Dry white is referred to as 'dry' or 'extra dry' – the English terms are used on labels in most countries. Traditional vermouth is made with white wine; red vermouth gets its hue from the herbs used for flavouring, as well as some caramelized sugar for colouring if necessary.

Many wonderful, small artisanal producers are popping up in the New World as well as in Europe today. These new companies may make vermouth in traditional styles, or with their own formulas:

recipes of wines, herbs, spices and production techniques that might be quite different from historic production. Each country or region has its own rules for vermouth labelling, and some of them can be quite broad. But if new producers don't want to be identified with a specific vermouth style from France or Italy or Spain, they don't have to be. This can make for fascinatingly creative vermouths. However, it can also make it difficult for bartenders to create drinks with these very original products: a mixologist must sample each vermouth, and then work out his or her own cocktail formula that melds well with each one. These are the pros and cons for each producer, who must choose either a variable artisanal style, or the standardized international style.

A Note on Bitterness

Some producers, both large and small, make a version of vermouth which is actually a 'bitter': a distillation of a fortified wine wherein herbs are used to create an extremely bitter flavour, and the alcohol percentage is usually significantly higher than that of vermouth. 'Bitters' (plural) are something completely different. They are herbal infusions used by the drop, as flavourings; the most famous one is Angostura bitters.

Sometimes a 'bitter' becomes confused with vermouth. For instance, the well-known Italian Punt e Mes is a genuine vermouth made in Piedmont, with a larger proportion of bitter herbal flavouring. On the other hand, Barolo Chinato, which is another bitter libation also from Piedmont, is not vermouth. It is in the 'bitter' category, which in Italian encompasses many different liqueur-style drinks that are known as *amari* (*amaro*, singular). The difference can be in the base wine and in the amount of bitter flavouring. Barolo Chinato producers, for example, use a base of Barolo, a red wine. They also aim for more of an emphasis on the bitterness, while true vermouth is a more complex melange of flavours ranging from sweet through herbal to bitter.

Unless the production method is known – or there is clear labelling – it is easy to confuse these preparations because a bottle of bitter may look like a vermouth and it may (or may not) contain similar herbs. In Italy, for instance, each region has its own preferred traditionally made, local bitter. In fact every village in the region may have a slightly different favourite preparation.

Bitter products are most often employed as *digestivos* in Italy or *digestifs* in France, which means they are traditional, well-respected aids to digestion; they are usually taken after the meal. Vermouth is served before the meal and if anything is considered to be an appetite stimulant, not a calming drink.

It's almost a matter of degree. But for the purposes of this book, the discussion here will be about fortified wines that self-identify as vermouth. For the reasons noted above, and because there are infinite numbers and styles of local 'digestive' bitters made with fortified wines and other types of alcoholic bases, this chapter will deal only with the larger categories of vermouth: red, *blanc* or *bianco* (sweet white) and extra dry (also known as dry white).

Italian and French History Intertwined

By the early 1800s vermouth's popularity had spread from Piedmont west to the southern Alpine region of France, where it was also produced by quite a few companies. Soon afterwards it spread to Spain, which mainly produced domestically consumed vermouths. It wasn't until about the year 2000 that vermouth began its current resurgence around the world.

But first, back to the origins of this drink. Distillation had become well known a few centuries before vermouth was created, and was popularized in Europe by the work of Arnaud de Villaneuve, who lived about AD 1240–1311. He was born in an area of Europe then dominated by the Crown of Aragon. This kingdom encompassed parts of several countries as we know them today, including southern France, southern Italy, northern and eastern Spain and the islands of Sardinia and Majorca. Villaneuve (also known as Villanova and a variety of other spellings) was famous throughout the kingdom, gaining celebrity at Montpellier and other universities where he taught and wrote about medicine and theology. Villaneuve is widely believed to be the originator of the concept of fortifying wine, using the Arab-originated process of distilling grapes, which he then added to local wine to make it stronger, mainly for medicinal purposes. Whether it was luck, skill or a combination of the two, under his ministrations Villaneuve's most notable patients did recover from their health problems. He became a doctor to kings and popes, moving among the kingdoms of Majorca and Aragon. Prolific in scientific research and theological exploration, he wrote dozens of books on both of these subjects, at least one of which was preserved for hundreds of years in the Vatican Library, copied over and over until the invention of the printing press, when it was printed and reprinted for centuries. According to legend, Villaneuve was on his way to cure another king when his ship went down off the coast of Genoa around 1311. Luckily, his process of fortifying wine was not lost at sea.

These events happened in the very region where vermouth was born: in what is now southern France, northern Italy and a section of northern Spain that includes Catalonia. Shortly after the achievements of Arnaud de Villaneuve became known, winemakers began to use distilled spirits to 'fortify' wine – literally to make the wine stronger, so it would be more palatable after long ocean voyages when wines were exported from France, Portugal or Spain to England, the Netherlands and other countries too far north to be able to grow their own wine grapes. At the same time, herbalists and doctors were experimenting with distillation

Arnaud de Villaneuve, a doctor, philosopher and professor who lived and worked mainly in Mediterranean areas that are now part of France and Spain, is credited as producing the first medicinal distillations in Europe, around AD 1300.

ARNALDVS — VILLANOVANVS —

to extract medicinal elements from various plants. They could either add the herbs to the fermented grapes or grain while they were distilling them, or they could distil the herbs separately, then add them to a wine or spirit. They also created more palatable medicines by adding sweeteners and mixing the herbal extracts into wine.

In other parts of the world and centuries earlier, in China, ancient Egypt, classical Greece and Rome, a rudimentary distillation process was known, as was the popular addition of herbs and spices to wine. There is currently some debate about which culture was the first to make flavoured drinks with a base of wine or brandy, but that discussion is best left to archaeologists and ethnologists at this point. The concern here centres not on what happened thousands of years ago in different continents, but on the drink called vermouth, and when and how it came into being.

One theory of the invention of vermouth credits a sixteenth-century inhabitant of Piedmont. This man, who was named Alessio or d'Alessio, produced a locally made drink enhanced with worm-wood (*Wermut* in German) which was similar to a popular medicinal wine in Germany. Alessio had apparently learned about this wine while visiting Bavaria, and brought the concept back to Piedmont. His beverage was not necessarily a fortified wine, and it was taken as a medicine. However, a modern u.s. company, Tempus Fugit Spirits, now produces several vermouths with the brand name Alessio in tribute to this historical figure.

Whether or not Alessio contributed to its invention, today we would still say that vermouth is from Italy, and specifically from the city of Turin in Piedmont. So it's not a coincidence that Turin is also currently a centre for the European commercial revival of vermouth. This Italian city remains the spiritual, and actual, home of vermouth – even though the countries we now know as France and Italy did not have the same borders a few hundred years ago. At the time that vermouth was first popularized, Turin was part of the Kingdom of Savoy, which encompassed the southeastern part of France now known as Savoie, as well as the northwestern region of

Italy that is now called Piedmont. Beginning in 1416, the dukes who ruled Savoy maintained Chambéry (which is now in France) as their capital city. In 1563 they shifted the capital to Turin.

In the early 1700s the Savoyard dukes also became rulers of the Kingdom of Sardinia. Through various conflicts and treaties, the province of Savoy itself became part of France for a while (1792–1815), but the Savoy kings consolidated their power and won it back. Then Savoy was deeded to France in 1860 when the Kingdom of Sardinia became part of the newly unified country of Italy. A ruler of the Kingdom of Sardinia, Victor Emmanuel II, was the first ruler of Italy; in fact he was instrumental in brokering the unification.

As it happens, a Savoyard king is also considered directly responsible for the popularity of vermouth; this was Victor Emmanuel II's father, King Carlo Alberto, in 1840. At that point in time, vermouth had become such a popular drink that the local producers deemed it necessary to arrange the protection of a king to keep it authentic. But before that, someone had to actually invent the fashionable Italian drink called vermouth.

Currently, prevalent belief – buoyed by the Carpano vermouth company today – is that the inventor of modern vermouth was Antonio Benedetto Carpano. He came from a rural area in northeast Piedmont so of course he would have been familiar with regional mountain herbs and herbal drinks. Carpano went to Turin seeking work, and found a job as an assistant in a wine shop in the centre of Turin, a shop owned by a man named Marendazzo.

The shop was located in a central plaza that is now called Piazza del Castello, which is still considered a chic meeting place. In the late 1700s this is where the nobility and other fashionable people gathered over drinks and small bites in the late afternoon, to discuss the topics

Since the invention of vermouth, people have been meeting at Piazza del Castello to share news of the day over an aperitif.

of the day. In 1786 Carpano began to produce a fortified wine that included many local herbs as well as quite a number of international spices that were available in the sophisticated city of Turin.

As the story goes, for the base of his drink Carpano used a good-quality wine made with white grapes grown nearby. When he started selling this wine to customers at Marendazzo's wine shop, it quickly caught on. It became a very stylish drink for the nobility, especially when the local Savoy ruler decided to replace his traditional preprandial Rosolio cordial with Carpano's drink. Carpano and Marendazzo likely chose a German term for this new drink in reference to a familiar German medicinal wine made with wormwood and/or in tribute to the Savoyard connection with the German nobility of the Holy Roman Empire; they called their drink simply 'Wermut' or 'Vermut'.

Wermut is the German word for the herb wormwood (also known as artemisia), which was an important element in the original formula, and remains a key ingredient in today's European vermouths. Several different species of artemisia grow wild along roads and pathways in the hills and mountains in various areas of Europe, including in the Alps and their foothills in France, Italy and

Switzerland. Artemisia is also a major ingredient in absinthe, the notorious liqueur that was also invented around the same time – in the late eighteenth century – in artemisia-growing regions on the border of Switzerland and France.

As mentioned earlier, people had been mixing herbs into wine and brandy for centuries to create medicines. They added sweetening, too, to make the medicines more palatable. A sweet-and-bitter concoction of herbs, spices, wine and brandy was not an unusual drink for this region at that time. Carpano's beverage became popular perhaps not because it was so different, but because it was a drink with familiar flavours. Whether it was the excellent ingredients and superior complexity of Carpano's beverage that led to its success, or the fortunate timing and location of his invention, will never be known. Probably all these elements contributed, along with pricing

Artemisia, a herb that grows wild in mountainous regions of Europe, is one of the signature flavourings of classic vermouths.

that was reasonable enough so that not only kings and dukes but many prosperous citizens of Turin could afford to indulge.

As the fame of Carpano's vermouth increased, other people began to jump on the bandwagon. Distillers, winemakers and pharmacists realized they had the means to create their own vermouths, especially those who were familiar with their native herbs, had access to local wines and were located along the same European spice routes. During the early 1800s, vermouth's fame – and production – spread to France, while in Turin, several other companies as well as individuals began to make vermouth.

In 1786 Antonio Benedetto Carpano invented vermouth, and the Carpano company still produces vermouth based on his formula.

It is said that by 1837, King Carlo Alberto's chef had created a vermouth especially for the king to sip before a meal, and that the king put out a decree in 1840 giving vermouth di Torino its own designated protection of origin status. Unfortunately, this must have disappeared in the unification of Italy twenty years later, but there is in existence today a vermouth company called Carlo Alberto in honour of this king. The founder of this company used the recipe of Carlo Alberto's chef – who was his father – to start a company that made wine, vermouth and liqueurs in 1871. In 2016 the company was relaunched by the chef's great-grandson to produce 'Riserva Carlo Alberto' vermouths in very elaborate glass bottles. The company also distributes a 'Punt e Mes' vermouth, with more of vermouth's characteristic bitter herbs added.

Several world-famous vermouth companies got their start in Turin in the immediate aftermath of Carpano. The prominent Cinzano company claims it originated before then, specifically in 1757, which refers to the fact the Cinzano brothers were experimenting with aromatized wines in the mid-1700s. The Cinzano family were appointed confectioners to the Royal Court of Savoy

View of a typical city in the vermouth-producing area a century ago. This is Vittorio Alfieri boulevard and piazza in the Italian city of Asti.

in 1776, which meant they supplied it with candies, flavourings, jams and marmalades, decorations and distilled products. However, they really began to produce vermouth commercially sometime in the 1800s. In 2014, to highlight the longevity and tradition of the Cinzano brand, the company came out with a 'Casa Cinzano 1757' range. These vermouths are described as 'small batch, handcrafted' and 'inspired by historical recipes', and they tend to be relatively more complex and intensely flavoured.

From Drops to Glasses to Bottles

Vermouths are sold in full bottles (750 ml), half bottles (375 ml) and sometimes 50 cl (500 ml) sizes in different parts of the world, depending on the cultural use of the vermouth. In the U.S., for example, where many people use only a few drops of vermouth in modern Martinis, the half-bottles of extra dry vermouth are quite useful for home bars. Larger bottles are much more practical in other countries where the vermouth itself is the aperitif – served over ice, perhaps with a garnish of citrus fruit or zest.

Just as wine glasses have become the vessel of choice for tasting everything from still to sparkling wines at wineries, today's vermouth producers offer tastes in wine glasses as well. And when making cocktails, it is no longer *de rigueur* to serve certain drinks only in certain glassware. Vermouth cocktails of all types are now being offered to customers in all different styles of glasses.

When storing vermouth, the popular myth is that it will last forever on your drinks cabinet shelf. While some of the more oxidized vermouths will last longer after being opened, vermouth is not shelf-stable indefinitely. Especially with the newer, more artisanal, craft-beverage style formulas, it is best to store vermouth in the refrigerator after opening the bottle, if it is not going to be consumed within a few weeks.

The Aperitif

By the time vermouth became popular, its value was more in the nature of a recreational beverage than a herbal remedy. That being said, vermouth was often thought of as a before-dinner appetite stimulant – as it is to this day, in many countries. Vermouth is an aperitif, a word that derives from the same root as 'appetite' and 'appetizer'. The word 'aperitif' itself is a relatively new invention: *apéritif* is a French word that only began to be used in English in 1894, according to the Merriam-Webster dictionary. It is derived from a Latin verb meaning 'to open' – signifying the launch of the evening or the appetite for dinner, or both. This concept came into fashion with the ritual of having a drink of vermouth before dinner in the vermouth-producing cities of Italy and France, and has spread around the world from there.

Though the appearance of a bottle of vermouth implies aperitif time in many regions, in Spain it actually *means* aperitif time. The term *fer un vermouth* describes meeting up with friends and family to have a drink (often vermouth, but not always) with a few tapas or *pintxos*, in order to stimulate one's appetite for dinner. It can be an evening and/or a Sunday noon custom, depending on the region of Spain.

Spain also has its own extremely vibrant vermouth culture. Vermouth *rojo* (red) tends to be preferred by Spanish consumers, but it has a different flavour profile from the Italian or French reds. It is sweet, and it has more Mediterranean herbs and slightly saline notes. Much of the Spanish vermouth is made from local white wines in the Catalonia or Rioja areas.

Creating Vermouth

Vermouth is a wine that is fortified and aromatized. This means that additional alcohol in the form of a neutral spirit such as an unaged brandy or vodka has been added to the wine – along with essences of herbs and spices, flowers and fruits, which is the meaning of 'aromatized' here. The added alcohol is usually made from distilled grape material (such as fermented grapes or grape pomace), though in some areas it can be made with other fruit pomace, or wheat or other grains. The herbs and spices are macerated in alcohol and then added. Both of these – the alcohol itself and the herb and spice extracts – contribute to the overall percentage of alcohol in the wine.

Even for red (*rosso* or *rouge*) vermouth, the base wine is generally white. It is most common for this vermouth to be made from grapes that are turned into wines without strong flavours, though the grapes themselves may be aromatic. These include fairly 'neutral' grapes similar to those used to make Cognac or Armagnac, for example, such as Trebbiano, Malvasia, various types of Moscato (also known as Muscat), Colombard and other local white grapes from the region wherever the vermouth is produced. Sometimes a small portion of the grapes are added in *mistelle* (unfermented grape juice) form, which adds freshness and fruit to the finished product.

In addition to the choice of wines and spirits, the selection of herbs and spices is critical. Recently, new processes are being used to prepare them. In white vermouths, it is common to have as many as fifteen or twenty herbs. In red vermouths, the number can rise to 25, 35 or even more. Each one must be obtained from the purest sources, and must be imported and stored correctly, because vermouth can be produced at any time of the year.

Then comes the most difficult part: the extraction. Each herb and spice must be handled in a specific manner. Every vermouth producer has their own version of the process. Some producers add whole herbs and spices to the alcohol or directly to the wine or *mistelle*. Now that consumer demand is for finer, more artisanal and distinctive vermouths, the bar is being set higher. Today, producers are using more individualized extractions so they can determine the precise number of days, weeks or months to optimize the flavours and aromas they are looking for. Once the extraction is complete, the herbed or spiced liquid is run through a press and then strained. With dozens of herbs and spices to work with, this calls for increasingly meticulous methods and techniques.

The herb known as artemisia or wormwood provides one of the most distinctive aromas in classic vermouth. The bitterness comes from cinchona bark; this is called *cina* in Italian, and is the same bark from which quinine is extracted. Gentian is also important, as are a host of other spices, herbs, flowers and fruit, both local and exotic, including anise, cardamom, cassia bark, cinnamon, cloves, coriander, elderflower, germander, ginger, lavender, mace, marjoram, nutmeg, orange peel, orris root, rose, rhubarb, saffron, vanilla and violet.

Colour in red vermouths mainly comes from herbs and spices, but caramelized sugar may also be used for colouring. For sweetening, beet sugar is common in many parts of Europe while in other areas cane sugar or concentrated wine grape juice are allowed. The Carpano vermouth website has a short summary definition according to EU regulations: 'In order to be classed as a vermouth, it must be composed of at least 75% of wine, have a minimum alcoholic strength by volume of 14.5% or more and a maximum alcoholic strength by volume of less than 22% and must contain Artemisias, which are its characterizing elements.'

In other countries, vermouth standards may be administered by their domestic trade bodies. For example, in the U.S., vermouth is not required to have wormwood. In fact, wormwood is considered so dangerous that quantities must be kept extremely low and thujone levels (a component of wormwood) must be tested and listed as a specific ingredient. It's likely that a fabled, hundred-year-old fear of absinthe has contributed to this fear of wormwood in the U.S. – and perhaps in other countries. In fact, it has since been proven that much of the reported problem with absinthe in the early 1900s had to do with impurities in the alcohol and other ingredients, and with over-consumption too, not with the wormwood itself.

Artisanal producers today are bending the rules, changing the wines, the herbs, the spices and even the production methods. So when tasting at a small producer, it's important to note that the intent can be as significant as the finished product.

Branding Vermouth

In the early twentieth century, vermouth culture was going strong. The First World War put a dampener on lifestyle and entertainment in many parts of the world, but in the area around Turin, vermouth was an integral part of Italian everyday life. The Italian Futurists (1909–18) seized upon vermouth cocktails as one aspect of their new movement. Roberto Bava of Cocchi vermouth has been researching Futurism and published a book about its history, including its cocktails, which the Futurists called *polibibite* because as staunch Italians, they refused to use the American term for mixed drinks.

Then came international trade interruptions, including Prohibition in the U.S., the Great Depression of the 1930s, the Spanish Civil War and the Second World War. Through it all, a few companies remained strong, including France's Noilly Prat and Italy's Martini (known as Martini & Rossi in the U.S.) and Cinzano (which, incidentally, is pronounced 'chin-ZAH-noh').

To many people around the world the name Cinzano means 'vermouth', much as the brand name Kleenex is used as a synonym for 'facial tissue' in the U.S. Currently, Cinzano is sold in fifty countries

Some of the impressive number of botanicals used in the production of vermouth; this display is at Cocchi Vermouth di Torino.

around the world, in Eastern and Western Europe, North and South America. According to the company, the familiar Italian drinking toast *cin cin* (pronounced 'chin chin') developed from Cinzano's very memorable commercials and jingles of the mid-twentieth century.

For the past hundred years, Cinzano has become well known for its artistic posters and advertisements and for sponsoring sporting events from cycling to power boat racing. The company also produced popular branded accessories like the triangular ashtrays that became ubiquitous in European cafes in the 1950s and '60s – and which were nicked and brought home from Italy as prized souvenirs by so many U.S. and UK travellers. Even more coveted today are the Cinzano café umbrellas, which are too unwieldy to pilfer; fortunately, they are now available online.

In 1999 Cinzano was acquired by Gruppo Campari, producers of Campari and other legendary Italian drinks, and the company has continued to expand its worldwide media presence and distribution. Historically, Argentina, with its extensive population of Italian

This lively poster from the early 20th century sends out the message 'Cinzano Vermouth rules the world!'

immigrants, considers Cinzano its native brand; its red vermouth has been distributed in Argentina for over a hundred years. Cinzano is fairly new in Russia, having appeared around a decade ago, and the preference there is to sip the dry white vermouth. In China Cinzano is quite new; there and in Hong Kong, Shanghai, Singapore and Taiwan, vermouth cocktails are in an introductory stage, and are growing in popularity.

Another classic Italian vermouth with a genuine worldwide presence is Martini & Rossi, which was founded in 1863 and is still headquartered in its historic stucco-walled production facility near the railway station in the city of Pessione, outside of Turin. At that time it was known as Martini and Sola (technically Martini, Sola & Cia). Founder Alessandro Martini had been working at an existing vermouth bottling company, but he was very entrepreneurial and decided to pursue his own vermouth production. He partnered with Teofilo Sola as his finance director and brought in Luigi Rossi, a vermouth maker from Turin. Not long after they started Sola died at a young age, after which the company name was changed to Martini & Rossi.

Martini & Rossi has proudly been headquartered in the town of Pessione in Piedmont since 1863. Visitors can tour the original buildings and sample cocktails there by appointment.

The company moved to its current location in 1864 because the owners 'took a long view' of their future, as current Martini & Rossi employees describe it. Surrounding the town are vineyards, which the original owners eyed for the local wines they would use in their products. And with a railway nearby they figured they could easily get their product out to the world – which is exactly what they did. Martini & Rossi vermouth was exported to the u.s. as early as 1867. Company founders also concentrated on appearing at international exhibitions and entering contests in order to create awareness of their product and then advertise their vermouth's medal-winning quality. And it worked. By 1903 Martini & Rossi vermouth was recognized in seventy countries. Incidentally, in most countries the company became known simply as 'Martini', while in the u.s. it was always called 'Martini & Rossi' to differentiate the vermouth itself from the very popular Martini cocktail.

Martini & Rossi also promoted its vermouths through lifestyle campaigns with film stars of the day, and through sportsmen who were at least as famous as movie stars during the first part of the twentieth century. Martini sponsored horse races, sailing and golf events, and in 1968 even had its own automobile racing team. Beginning in 1948, they created *terrazzas* in the most happening urban areas around the world: invitation-only event spaces where the rich and famous could enjoy cocktails in cities including Paris, London, Geneva, Genoa and São Paulo. In Milan they hosted celebrities from the Italian cinema; there are two *terrazza* spaces still in operation in Italy today, and the company does pop-ups in various locations.

In Piedmont they have maintained a 'Casa Martini' at their Pessione headquarters since 1864. Advertised as a short train ride from Turin, today Casa Martini encompasses a bar, a museum and an event space, where tours are offered every day, and mixology and vermouth masterclasses every week. Today the Martini store also offers sportswear, watches, luggage, racing helmets and other gear, both at the company and online.

There is nothing more classic than a Martini cocktail, whether it is made in the traditional manner with gin, or the modern style with vodka.

Globally, one of the most well-distributed vermouths is Gancia, a mid-level vermouth company with an extensive heritage in the area. The company was established in 1850 and moved from Turin to its current location, near the railway line in Canelli, in 1866. One of the brothers of 'Fratelli Gancia' (as the company was then called) was a vermouth maker from Turin who had gone to France to learn how to make sparkling wine, and this is what Gancia first became known for: the introduction of an Italian champagne-style wine made with local grapes in Piedmont. Shortly thereafter the company is recorded as producing its own formula of white vermouth called 'vermouth Bianco', a sweeter riff on the French-style extra dry white

Cinzano vermouths at Dolce & Gabbana's Bar Martini in Milan, Italy.

One of many special cocktail recipes, this one with Vermouth Ambrato, at Casa Martini in the Martini & Rossi headquarters in Pessione, Italy.

vermouth – which the owner had most likely experienced on his travels in France.

In the 1920s Gancia opened an office in Marseille to capture more of the French market, and to facilitate exports by sea. After the Second World War the company launched Gancia Rosso vermouth on its one hundredth anniversary. In addition to innovative posters, the company continued to show its commitment to promotion with lavish campaigns including a ski-jumping trophy (started in 1934) and contests to win cars. The prize in 1951 was a Lancia car. During the year 1956 they gave away one Fiat Millecento car every month.

Ever conscious of its history, in 2003 the company applied for UNESCO World Heritage status for its extensive underground wine cellars; this was granted in 2008. Currently the company is effectively owned by Russian Standard, a well-known Russian vodka production company, which acquired a majority position in 2011, and in 2013 increased its ownership to 95 per cent.

Countless vermouth production companies were founded in the Torino-Asti area at the end of the nineteenth century. One of the most notable was established by Giulio Cocchi (pronounced KOH-kee) in 1891. He was also the inventor of the Americano cocktail. The Cocchi company established its own bars – technically 'authorized

resellers' – in major cities in the area during the height of vermouth's popularity. Before the First World War Cocchi had a dozen bars in Piedmont, along with a couple in Africa and South America; the latter were situated in two of the most exciting, exotic cities of the early twentieth century, Addis Ababa and Caracas. The Cocchi Bar in Asti is the only one still called by that name; the three others still in existence have had slight name changes to Bar Barolino Cocchi in Turin, Bar Barolino Chinato Cocchi in Savona and Bar Barolino in Levanto.

The name Cocchi is also significant because the current owner, Roberto Bava, is the driving force behind the resurrection of the important designation 'vermouth di Torino', an appellation which was ratified by the Italian government in March 2017. At that time, there were less than a dozen members of this prestigious association; it included the largest as well as the most historic producers, and newer artisanal producers as well.

The Bava family is also revitalizing a vermouth di Torino with a French name, Chazalettes. The French Chazalettes family moved from Chambéry to Turin in 1860. Clemente Chazalettes worked at Martini & Sola (which later became Martini & Rossi) before starting his own 'Les Chazalettes' vermouth company in 1876. It was extremely successful, and by 1907, Chazalettes became official suppliers to Queen Margherita and the Savoy princess Laetitia Bonaparte. Chazalettes' Turin production facility was destroyed by

Giulio Cocchi's original vermouth factory in Piedmont, Italy, established in 1891.

bombs during the Second World War, then rebuilt. But the company eventually stopped making vermouth in the 1970s, presumably because of lower demand, though they continued producing amari and other liqueurs for some time.

A few years ago, Roberto Bava and his daughter Francesca (of Cocchi vermouth) happened to be introduced to the last surviving director of the family business, Giovanni Chazalettes. He told them he regretted his company's shutting down its vermouth production, so the Bavas began working with Giovanni's recipes in order to create a vermouth in the style of the original Chazalettes. In its heyday, Les Chazellettes vermouths were customized for each export market: more alcohol was used in vermouths shipped to the farthest ports; vermouth was formulated to be conveyed to South America in casks and bottled there to avoid breakage; there was more orange flavouring for German palates, and so on. So the task now is to amalgamate the various Les Chazalettes formulas and create consistent, modern vermouths in the traditional styles.

Not far from Turin, Italy, the small town of Cocconato is now the headquarters of two founding members of the new vermouth di Torino association: Cocchi and Les Chazellettes.

The Bavas have longevity in the area, along with their newer production experience. The family has been growing wine grapes in Piedmont since 1682. Recent generations modernized the family business by bottling and selling their own wines, instead of just growing grapes for others. The current Bava winery is located next to a railway, like many other forward-thinking wine and vermouth producers. Roberto's father also merged with (basically acquired) the Cocchi company in 1978; Cocchi makes vermouth as well as Barolo Chinato and other regional specialities. At that time, the Cocchi plant was located in Asti; about fifteen years ago it was moved to the Bava winery property in the tiny village of Cocconato, located between Turin and Asti. Today, the Bava/Cocchi company works sustainably, with solar power. It also has a new seminar building constructed with a bar, kitchen and classroom, in which bartenders are educated about the brand and its products, and the Cocchi heritage is promoted and contributed to.

Another significant company in the area is Tosti, formerly known as Bosca. The name was changed in the late twentieth century by the current owner's parents because they felt Bosca was too common a name in this area. The Bosca family still runs the business, which began seven generations ago with vineyard ownership. They made wine for themselves and later started bottling and selling it,

The villages and countryside in the region where vermouth di Torino is now produced.

as was the case with many local grape-growing families. Vermouth came even later; the current company director Giovanni Bosca believes that his grandfather began to produce it seriously between the two world wars. Vermouth now makes up about 30 per cent of Tosti's production. A few years ago Tosti rededicated its vermouth line to re-creating the vermouth style of the 1930s, with a base of local Trebbiano wine, more local herbs and fine imported spices. Co-director Mariacristina Castelletta now dreams of creating a herb garden for visitors at the plant in Canelli.

Also located in this area between Asti and Turin is the noteworthy Quaglia company. The current owner is Carlo Quaglia, great-grandson of the Giuseppe Quaglia who, in 1906, acquired a distillery called Castelnuovo Don Bosco, which had been founded in 1890. The Quaglias proceeded to produce vermouth, Barolo Chinato and other drinks. The company became famous with its highly respected Berto brand, which debuted in 1930. Now Berto has a rival in popularity within its own company, because a few years ago Carlo formed an association with the Jerry Thomas Speakeasy in Rome to produce the chic Del Professore line of vermouths. On

Display of high-end bottles at the shop of cult favourite Vermouth del Professore.

a given day, Carlo can be found quietly minding the store, literally standing behind the counter in his library-esque little shop packed with excellent vermouths – which is not easy to find, at the end of a narrow lane in the tiny municipality of Castelnuovo Don Bosco, close to 30 kilometres (18 mi.) from Turin.

Moving into France

As mentioned earlier, both Turin and Chambéry were capitals of the Savoy Kingdom at different times during its centuries of existence. The relationship endures to this day; hundreds of years later Chambéry and Turin are still linked from their Savoyard time, when they were both on a trade route from Italian Mediterranean ports to northern cities, and because they were separated from the rest of Europe by the Southern Alps. One of the major producers of French vermouth, Pierre-Olivier Rousseaux, president of Dolin Vermouth in Chambéry, points to this geographical barrier to explain why in Lyon there is essentially still no vermouth cocktail culture, even though the city is barely an hour-and-a-half's drive from Chambéry. Even now, many people from the French town of Chambéry do not visit Lyon when they are seeking the benefits of a large city for anything from personal shopping to commercial business dealings, but rather habitually go to Turin in Italy. Nowadays there are highways and railways throughout France, of course, but provincial memories last a long time.

Chambéry may be little known outside its region at present, but in the nineteenth century it was a centre for vermouth production in France. Producers in Chambéry created and defined the French style of dry white vermouth (known as 'extra dry'), which was quite different from the Italian sweet red style. By the mid- to late 1800s there were several very active vermouth companies in the area. Recently, the founder of the Chambéry vermouth industry was one of the few left: Dolin, founded in 1821. The company remained in their original location near the railway station until very recently, when the city required manufacturers to leave the centre of town and move to a modern industrial park a few kilometres away.

Rediscovered (and revered) by mixologists early in the twenty-first century, Dolin was the first vermouth company established in Chambéry. It was founded by Joseph Chavasse, a medicinal herbalist, which means he functioned as a cross between a pharmacist and a doctor. Chavasse practised in the nearby town of Les Échelles. On a visit to Turin, Chavasse encountered vermouth di Torino – herbs and spices in a fortified wine – and decided that when he went home he would create his own version, vermouth de Chambéry, which he did. The company name was changed to Dolin after his daughter married Hyppolite Dolin and the younger couple took over the business. In 1830 they relocated to Chambéry because it was a larger city, a *carrefour alpin* (Alpine merchant corridor) through the lower Alps. Dolin Vermouth became popular quite quickly, and this spawned the growth of a whole new vermouth sector in Chambéry. By the end of the nineteenth century there were half a dozen more producers there, including Richard, Comoz, Reynard and Routin. Comoz was known as the creator of the white, sweet style of vermouth called *blanc* or *bianco*, as an alternative to the very dry original Chambéry white vermouth.

At that time in history each region of France had its own locally popular aperitif. For example, Cynar was consumed in northwest France, pastis in the southern part of the country, and vermouth in the French Alpine region. Dolin Vermouth was also exported very successfully to the UK and the U.S. The Dolin headquarters today displays a medal awarded to Mme Dolin at the Philadelphia Exposition of 1876.

This happy state of affairs lasted into the early twentieth century, until an unrelated political action precipitated the beginning of a drastic downturn in the French vermouth industry. This was the institution of the first official holiday policy for workers in France: the government mandated that each worker would have a week of paid holiday every year. Many of the French would journey south,

This Dolin Vermouth poster from the early 20th century captures the aesthetic of the time and place, and suggests the relaxing and revitalizing powers of vermouth.

and that's where they discovered pastis, which they brought back home to remind them of their wonderful holidays.

Pastis as an aperitif spread throughout France, and since that time, regional aperitifs of all types began to take a back seat to that new national favourite. Americans didn't help the vermouth cause, either. Though vermouth had become a mainstay of cocktails in the U.S., when servicemen came to France to fight in the First and Second World Wars, they brought their own taste for whiskey and it spread to the French. Vermouth soon became only a regionally consumed aperitif in France, confined to the Alpine region south of Lyon and just west of the Italian border (although it remained popular in nearby Switzerland and Italy).

The Dolin family didn't weather this decline of the French vermouth business very well, and in 1914 the company was acquired by the Sevez family, who ran the *épicerie fine* (delicatessen) company that supplied herbs and spices to Dolin. The current owners of Dolin are fifth-generation Sevez family members. The stepfather of Dolin director Pierre-Olivier Rousseaux was a Sevez, and Pierre-Olivier's wife is also from the Sevez family.

In the 1970s Rousseaux's stepfather was seriously considering the question of whether or not to continue Dolin's vermouth production. The company sold vermouth regionally and in the UK, but they were getting by mainly on their production of local liqueurs, including the important local favourite génépy, which is made with the hard-to-find flowers of a rare, wild Alpine artemisia; they also made a profitable line of fruit syrups for flavourings, which the company still produces under the brand name Marie Dolin.

Around the same time, Dolin also acquired the Bonal Quinquina (bitter aperitif) business but in the end they decided to persevere with vermouth as well. Luckily, in the early 2000s, the growing mixology movement discovered Dolin and began to champion this brand as an artisanal vermouth that added depth and complexity to cocktails.

Dolin remains a small operation, still housed in Chambéry. In fact, today the Dolin company has only twenty employees. Their vermouth was originally based on Savoie wine only, but today it is made with wine made from Ugni Blanc (also known as Trebbiano)

Historical bottles of vermouth produced around Chambéry, France, displayed at the offices of Dolin Vermouth.

grapes that are sourced nearby. There are seventeen herbs and spices in the Dolin dry white vermouth variety, and 34 in the (sweet) *blanc* and *rouge*. Dolin is also refining their process of herbal extractions along with other upgrades to its vermouth production.

Dolin also acquired the rights to the groundbreaking, historic Comoz vermouth *blanc* recipe, which uses herbs and spices different from Dolin's. After a full year of experimental batches, they finalized the production and began to release Comoz vermouth in 2018.

The other major producer still making vermouth de Chambéry is Routin, founded by Philibert Routin in 1883. Routin made the French-style dry white vermouth, as well as the *rouge* (red) vermouth and other liqueurs and flavoured syrups. Like Dolin, the production of fruit syrups and the local génépy liqueur helped the company survive the ups and downs of vermouth's popularity. (In fact, génépy remains a huge regional business, extremely popular among winter sports enthusiasts, selling well in the wine shops and restaurants of nearby world-famous ski resorts such as Grenoble and Chamonix.)

In the 1930s there were a dozen vermouth producers in Chambéry; by the end of the Second World War there were only two left. After Routin founder Philibert's death, his children ran the company until 1938, when the family died out and the Clochet family acquired it. They retained the Routin name, and kept the business going during the difficult years of the Second World War, when women had to replace men in the workforce of the production plant. The company then consisted of three divisions: a flavoured syrup department; Routin vermouth; and the distillery for liqueur production, which was called Montania.

In 2012 the Clochet family sold to a group of investors. The company, which continues to make vermouth as well as distilled products and flavourings, is now officially called Distillerie des Alpes. (The flavoured syrup division is now called 1883.) This can be confusing when searching for vermouth producers, but Routin seems aware of this and they have been working on their branding and exports. In

2015 they restarted the production of vermouth *blanc*, which they had not made for decades. They had noticed that newer consumers were looking for more light, sweet beverages; not everyone appreciated the arresting bitterness of the traditional dry white – or even the *rouge* – vermouths.

Routin uses local wine for its vermouth base: wine made from the little-known Savoie white grape called Jacquère. For herbs and spices, they use local artemisia in their total of 24 plants for the *rouge*, eighteen for the *blanc* and seventeen for the dry white. Like most European vermouth producers, they use non-GM beet sugar for sweetening.

And there is one more important French vermouth, the most prominent worldwide French brand, Noilly Prat. In 1813 Joseph Noilly, a herbalist in Lyon, heard about vermouth and decided to produce his own version. Demand grew so fast that he quickly moved the company to the port of Marseille. Joseph Noilly's son Louis partnered with Claude Prat to start up their export business in the 1850s, and within a few years these vermouths were known in bars from San Francisco to Sydney to Singapore.

In 1850 Louis also set up a production plant in the small (and confusingly named) seaport town of Marseillan, 200 km (125 mi.) west of Marseille. This town is also one of the termini of the Canal du Midi, which made it an important centre for commerce through the nineteenth century and into the twentieth. Marseillan became Noilly Prat's sole production facility and headquarters in the mid-1970s – though the buildings do have a much older feel to them. Today the town of Marseillan is known as a place where the French go on holiday in the summertime. Out of season it is a classic, charmingly old-fashioned little port city, with sailboats bobbing gently at their moorings alongside lichened stone docks, only a few metres away from the headquarters of one of the most famous vermouth companies in the world.

Some of the Noilly Prat vermouth is made with white wines from Andalusia, specifically a Moscato *mistelle*. Two native white wines

For over a century, Noilly Prat has been shipping their vermouths from their headquarters in the small coastal town of Marseillan, France.

from nearby are also used to make different styles of vermouth: Picpoul de Pinet and Clairette d'Adissan. These wines are placed in barrels that were formerly used for sherry, Scotch whisky, port or cognac. The wines are aged outside for a full year, placed in rows in an impressively large square in the middle of the production plant in Marseillan, to experience sun, rain, heat, cold and even the occasional squall of seaspray. Some of the wine does evaporate; as everywhere, the normal amount of 'angel's share' is around 6 per cent, and the barrels are not topped up, meaning that the wines become oxidized. This enables them to age for longer, and this is part of Noilly Prat's signature taste in all of their vermouths.

Noilly Prat is very welcoming to visitors, with tours and cocktail-making classes going on nearly year-round. The company has always been successful at its commercialization, first with its vermouth formula and then with its exports. Though Noilly Prat's various vermouths may have been created to be marketed in different parts of the world in the past, at present there is more homogeneity in their international offerings. The company now produces four styles of vermouth. There is a comparatively rare *ambré* (amber) style of vermouth, in addition to the Original Dry and Rouge, and Extra Dry. The *ambré* is a recent invention. Extra Dry was created at

Until relatively recently, Noilly Prat distilled all of the essences used in vermouth production at their headquarters in the south of France.

Noilly Prat's boutique and staff at their headquarters in Marseillan, France.

the end of the Second World War, basically for Americans to make cocktails with, so it is mainly sold at the factory or as an export; it was not created for the French palate. The Original Dry has been exported in 135 countries so far, and it is also used by many chefs in cooking.

The vermouths were originally fortified with distillate made on the property from local lemons and raspberries. This distillation continued until after Noilly Prat was acquired by the Bacardi company in 1992; the distillate is now made elsewhere in France (at the Bénédictine facility) but still with the same formula that includes lemons and raspberries.

Into the Twenty-first Century

Times were good for vermouth in France throughout the first half of the twentieth century. French vermouth was known worldwide, and often differentiated from Italian vermouth. In France, in 1930, vermouth de Chambéry had been granted protected status of origin designation, which was then called AO (Appellation d'Origine), a precursor to the French AOC (Appellation d'Origine Contrôllée) system of wine designations that came online in the 1930s. It appears that this designation had not been actively used for some time when, in 1990, European Union regulations required that all products submit applications to be reclassified under the EU's (renamed) system, which in French is called AOP (Appellation d'Origine Protégée) and is sometimes rendered in English as PDO (Protected Designation of Origin).

But with the downturn in production in the late twentieth century, no companies submitted the paperwork for vermouth de Chambéry. So as of 1 July 2000, vermouth de Chambéry lost its protected designation status. If and when the Chambéry producers apply to reinstate the designation, it would still take a number of years for the application to wend its way through the EU organization, now that the original status has lapsed.

Because of vermouth's growing popularity, this application would seem a likely occurrence – but it very well may not happen at this point in time. Apparently, there must be more than one producer, and a certain amount of uniformity of production in a specified region, in order for a product to be granted protected designation of origin status. This status defines the geographic area, manufacturing methods and other key elements required for the product.

The two current Chambéry producers do not see eye-to-eye on the elements required for this application, despite the fact that the 'vermouth de Chambéry' designation could be even more significant when recent developments in Italy are considered. In March 2017 vermouth di Torino received its designated status in Italy, from the Italian government. With the accession to this status in Italy, the Italian designation is unlikely to be to be challenged in the EU. The first president elected was Roberto Bava of Cocchi and the vice president was Giorgio Castagnotti of Martini & Rossi. The founding members of the vermouth di Torino Institute are Berto, Bordiga, Del Professore, Carlo Alberto, Carpano, Chazalettes, Cinzano, Giulio Cocchi, Drapò, Gancia, La Canellese, Martini & Rossi, Sperone, Vergnano and Tosti.

This is by no means a complete list of Italian vermouth producers, or even of vermouth di Torino producers. There are new ones cropping up all the time, at distilleries and at wineries. These include Montanaro in Piedmont, made at a hundred-year-old grappa distillery near Alba that decided to expand their production range. And La Canellese, a production facility in the countryside outside of near the city of Asti, also serves as a production facility for vermouth brands from Italy and other countries.

The 'vermouth di Torino' (also spelled 'vermout di Torino') designation celebrates the origins of vermouth in the city of Turin, and continues its formal status with the production rules by which the vermouth must be made. Specifically, it must be made in a designated area surrounding the cities of Turin and Asti, which are located in the Piedmont region of Italy.

Vermouth di Torino is made with white grapes grown around the town of Canelli and in other nearby vineyards in the Piedmont region of Italy.

Many small towns are included in this designated area, notably Canelli. This small city is located south of Asti and east of Alba – the two cities that also anchor Piedmont's famed wine production zone for the well-known red wines Barolo, Barbaresco, Dolcetto d'Alba and Ruché, and the white Roero and Moscato d'Asti wines. Today Canelli, with a population of only 10,000, is still a vibrant wine production-related industrial area, home to companies that produce labels, pallets, bottling machines and other supplies for winemakers who are headquartered nearby in Italy and in France.

One of the requirements of vermouth di Torino is that the grapes used to make the wine must be 75 per cent local – grapes such as Moscato, also used to produce Piedmont's well-known sparkling Moscato d'Asti. The town of Canelli is thought to be a primary source of the historically significant Moscato grape that is known in English as Muscat Canelli. The name 'Muscat Canelli' is familiar to grape suppliers, though the grape itself may be more widely known to others as Muscat à Petits Grains; this grape has been planted in many countries for centuries so it is likely that just the English name, not the grape itself, originated in the town of Canelli.

Several large vermouth producers relocated their production facilities to the Canelli area when they grew too big to be headquartered in Turin in the nineteenth century. At that time, there was a busy railway line that came through Canelli's industrial zone. That rail service has lapsed and the former railway stations stand as charming, yet tantalizingly closed, lovely old buildings. However, several of the largest vermouth producers, such as Martini & Rossi and Gancia, are still located in their original warehouse spaces near the railway line.

Further north, on the way from Asti to Turin, the tiny town of Cocconato (population 1,600) is the current home of vermouth producers Cocchi and Les Chazalettes, as well as being the headquarters of the vermouth di Torino movement.

In Turin itself, there is currently only one vermouth producer, a new company established in 2012 called Drapò, a name that refers to the flag of Turin in the local dialect. This vermouth developed from the owner's hobby, with a family recipe from 1950 that grew so popular among his friends that he decided to create his own

Martini & Rossi's extensive vermouth production plant with its own railway line in the city of Pessione in Piedmont, Italy.

production facility. The feel at Drapò is super-artisanal. The base wines of Trebbiano and Moscato are locally sourced, as are many of the aromatic elements. Fruit, flower, herb and spice extractions are being fine-tuned with micro-extractions, pressure extractions and barrel-ageing of flavouring essences. The entire facility is postmodern in design: a Tuscan-gold, retro-hued exterior, large warehouse spaces with cheerful red floors and bright colours everywhere. There is even a small bar/classroom area for educational events and masterclasses.

Spain's Strong Vermouth Culture

In Spain, vermouth was traditionally produced in the northeast, mainly in Catalonia, with a sub-region of producers in Rioja. Most Spanish vermouth was also consumed there, but the vermouth custom has spread throughout Spain, with bars in Madrid first joining this movement and, more recently, bars and sherry producers as far south as Jerez.

In Andalusia, where sherry comes from, they are using young sherries or wines that are made from the same grapes as the base for vermouths. Spanish producers tend to make sweet red (as well as some dry white) vermouths, along with some 'reserve' vermouths in the same categories. Lustau was the first large, sherry-producing company exporting vermouth to the U.S., and others are expected to follow this lead. Lustau's red vermouth is made with a base of its amontillado and Pedro Ximenez sherries, along with many fruits, flowers, herbs and spices traditionally used in vermouth.

From the north, one of Spain's most popular vermouths is Yzaguirre, which is also exported to the U.S. and UK. Miró is on the way, as is De Mueller's Iris vermouth. Other companies are beginning to export more, including Primitivo Quiles, Montana Perucchi, Destilerias Acha, Martinez Lacuesta and Padró.

Padró, for example, is a fairly typical story for a vermouth producer in northern Spain. Padró is a family company that started making vermouth in 1886 with the brand name Myrrha. It is located in Catalonia, in the heart of the vermouth production area, near the port of Tarragona. The family started delivering their products to local bars and shops that specialized in vermouth, which was becoming more and more popular in Spain. More recently, they have begun to produce a premium vermouth under the label Padró & Co.

Inland a few miles from Tarragona is the city of Reus, which became a centre for vermouth consumption in the 1860s, according to Spanish vermouth expert Joan Tàpias. By the end of the 1800s there were thirty companies producing fifty brands of vermouth in the Reus-Tarragona area. Tàpias describes these vermouths as weaker and sweeter than the Italian vermouths. It seems that most of the Spanish vermouths were consumed domestically, and though the industry was strong there, very little was known about it outside of Spain.

World wars and political constraints during most of the twentieth century conspired to keep Spain's vermouth production a secret from the rest of the world. But its popularity at home never waned. In fact, many bars began to produce their own barrels of vermouth, available to patrons by the glass or the bottle. Neighbourhood bodegas or *vermuterias* (vermouth bars) all had their own formulas, and local residents frequented their favourites. In cities from Madrid to Barcelona, this is still the case. Some small shops cater mainly to people who come by with their own bottles to fill; others function more like conventional bars where people stop in for a quick drink at the end of the day, before dinner.

A few years ago, Tàpias established his Museu del Vermut (vermouth museum) in Reus, as a home for his own collection of historic and rare vermouths, as well as hundreds of fun vermouth artefacts and posters. In addition, Tàpias produces his own red and white vermouths under the label 'Cori' in a joint venture with the nearby Miró company.

The museum also encompasses a *vermuteria*, which carries a plethora of vermouths from Reus and Catalonia in Spain, and from many different countries. Of course there is also a restaurant where delightful local snacks and lunches are served along with

Created in New York
in the late 19th century,
the Manhattan cocktail
is known worldwide.

the vermouths, because in Spain, all vermouth experiences are food-related. The expression *hacer un vermouth* (literally 'to make a vermouth') actually means a time to relax while sipping a vermouth aperitif – which is always served with some kind of tapas – before having a meal with friends and family. This was a popular custom for over a hundred years in Spain. It began to lag towards the end of the twentieth century, but it is now experiencing a wonderful revival concurrent with the global renaissance of vermouth.

In the u.s., as in other countries, there have always been large, commercial producers of all three styles of vermouth – though some that are labelled 'dry' seem to stray over the border into sweetness. Two of the largest producers in the world include Stock (now labelled Lionello, which is the first name of the founder) based in Italy and the Gallo company based in the u.s. They are readily available and useful. But the more exciting developments today are in artisanal vermouths, which are made in so many wine regions in so many countries that it is impossible to keep track of which winemakers and distillers have begun vermouth production.

Artisanal Vermouth Revival

The first artisanal vermouth of the modern era was the Quady Vya from Madera, California, which came on the market in 1998, cresting the global wave of mixology. Owner-winemaker Andrew Quady had researched vermouth as an oenology student and he was always open to experimenting with new products. He had a friend who owned an Italian restaurant in San Francisco, and the friend constantly bemoaned the fact that Americans were vermouth-adverse. In fact most u.s. drinkers considered vermouth a cheap and bad quality drink.

Quady thought he could do better, and he did, creating Vya white and red vermouths, with great complexity of aromas and flavours. He used local Pinot Grigio and Colombard, looking for freshness and 'grapey' aromas. He fortified and sweetened the vermouths with his Quady port-style and Muscat dessert wines. Bartenders found that the Vya vermouths improved their Martini and Negroni cocktails. Restaurant owners were intrigued by being able to use American-made products, in an era when the use of local food was on the ascendency. And the mixology movement took it from there.

There are more and more vermouth producers appearing all the time in California and in other states in the u.s., as well as in Australia, South Africa and anywhere in the New World where producers are inspired to create their own versions of this aromatized, fortified wine. And there is plenty of demand. Since the turn of the twenty-first century, mixologists have suddenly rediscovered vermouth, and are again featuring it in their new cocktails. The timing seems concurrent with the vermouth production revival, so it's difficult to say which came first. As sommeliers and bartenders started travelling more, they began to find more artisanal vermouths, *amari* and other liqueurs in small, regional hotels and restaurants, and they became inspired by the rare flavours and aromas they discovered there – a welcome change after having been brought up with only a couple of the lower-quality vermouths available.

Vermouths can provide several of the necessary elements in a cocktail: sweetness, bitterness and acidity. Classic vermouth cocktails include the Americano, the Martini, the Manhattan and the Negroni. In bars throughout the world today, bartenders are creating their own versions with locally sourced, artisanal flavours added to the celebrated original recipes. Thrilled by the cocktail world's interest, vermouth producers have also stepped up their game, delving into the past for original formulas from previous decades and centuries, adjusting their formulas for the modern palate, and using better-quality ingredients and processes: this is a stimulating time for vermouth!

2
Port

Rich, red and plummy, or elegantly spiced and tawny, port delivers an abundance of aromas and flavours. Embedded in drinks rituals for centuries, port wine consumption now ranges from a rite at the end of a formal dinner party to casual cocktails before or after a meal.

Yes, cocktails, both historic and modern. When Americans started making mixed drinks in the nineteenth century, they used the wines and spirits they were most familiar with as the bases of their drinks. The most popular were rum, brandy and port. Rum was excitingly tropical, brandy was known to be medicinal and port was considered strengthening, and it also had class – all good reasons to incorporate them into one's diet. This was well before any significant amounts of gin or vodka were imported, of course. Current mixologists, cresting a new wave of cocktail popularity in the twentieth century, have devoted themselves to re-creating the joys of early cocktails, and now it seems that every bartender worth their salt has several tempting port-based libations in their repertoire.

Historically, port has been one of the most revered and intimidating fortified wines in the Western world. It is revered because it's one of the finest long-ageing wines in the world, with great global appeal and significance; it is intimidating because it seemed there

Fresh fruit and ten-year-old tawny go well together in Warre's summery port cocktail.

was so much to learn about port before one could purchase knowledgeably and consume it appropriately. In actuality, those layers of port legends, vintages and styles do not need to stand between consumers and their port glasses today. Port is not a beverage to be conquered; it's to be sipped and appreciated.

Enlarging on the theme of conquest, it's interesting to note that this smooth and luscious beverage owes its very existence to war, to political as well as trade conquests and conflicts in Europe, beginning in the seventeenth century. England needed wine, and

France supplied it – except when the two nations were at war, which occurred on and off for several hundred years. That's when merchants and traders set up offices in Portugal, with its friendly Atlantic Ocean ports to the south of Spain and France. A new Anglo-Portuguese alliance was built upon long-standing treaties from the Middle Ages. At first, the British merchants imported the lighter, weaker wines of far northern Portugal, but these wines were harsh and unpalatable to the English. So the British began to source wines from inland along Portugal's Douro Valley. Later, they found the wines could be further strengthened (literally) by fortification, a benefit for both transportation and consumption.

The first port wine shipments to England began in earnest after the Anglo-Portuguese trade agreement of 1654 and a subsequent trade restriction between England and France later that century. British merchants sought hearty red wines from Portugal's Douro Valley and shipped them home, occasionally fortifying them with a bit of brandy or neutral spirits. But it wasn't until the second half of the eighteenth century that port evolved into its current style of a complex, fortified wine, long-ageing and highly sought after.

And so we have port, named for the Portuguese port it was shipped from. This is a very simplified version of port's history, with more to come.

How the Port Region and Industry Evolved

The grapes for port are grown in the Douro region of Portugal, a couple of hours' drive east of the city of Oporto, along the steep hillsides of the Douro River. (There has been some confusion about the name of the city where port wine shipping originated: is it Oporto or Porto? Historically, Oporto was in common usage until quite recently, when it seemed to dawn on English-speaking people that 'Oporto' actually means simply 'the port'. Today the shift to calling the city Porto is nearly complete. In terms of port wine, in Portugal it is known as *porto* while the British and Americans call it 'port';

other countries vary in their preferences.) The Douro River runs
east to west, originating in Spain, where it is called the Duero. It
is a powerful river that now has several energy-producing dams
in both countries. The Douro empties into the Atlantic Ocean just
beyond Oporto.

The region where port's grapes are grown is quite arid, with
extremes of heat in the summer and cold in the winter. It's so precipitous and inhospitable a terrain it is remarkable to think that
wine grapes have been grown there commercially for more than four
centuries. In the past it was several days' journey from Oporto to
the tiny villages and isolated *quintas* (farms or estates) of the Douro.
But the quality of the grapes made it all worthwhile.

There were more hurdles involved in getting the wine downriver
to where it was aged in the town across the river from Oporto. This
town, which was originally called Vila Nova de Gaia, is now known
simply as Gaia. There, ports were kept in storage buildings called
'port lodges' that were built on the quays along the banks of the
Douro River. The river's moderating influence helped to maintain
the wine in a more favourable environment for ageing: the lodges
were more humid and had more moderate year-round temperatures
than upriver where the grapes were grown.

Looking at the names of Portugal's port producers, there's something striking about them: so many of the names of the most famous
producers sound British. In fact, they are. The port industry as we
know it was essentially created by British traders, to supply British
markets in order to decrease dependence on French wines during
times of conflict from the Middle Ages on.

Going back to the beginning of winemaking in Portugal, the
Romans grew grapes there in the second century AD. Wine continued to be produced in the area until the Moorish domination of
the Iberian Peninsula, which began in AD 711. Portugal's Christian
monarchs, with the help of the English, reclaimed their lands in
1147 and established the country of Portugal in 1179. A significant
trade treaty was signed between Portugal and England in 1386, and

Port casks being prepared for shipment in Vila Nova de Gaia, across the Douro River from the city of Porto, 1835.

the two nations became profitable trading partners, with English codfish and Portuguese wine as the original cornerstones. However, the wines produced in northern and coastal Portugal were not great quality, and probably suffered further degradation during the time it took to ship them abroad. But English merchants had established themselves in Portugal, and along with merchants from other Northern European countries they continued to trade fish and wool for Portugal's fruit and olive oil, along with some wines.

By the first half of the sixteenth century, producers with wines from the Douro River Valley had begun to send their wines on the treacherous journey down the river to Oporto, where wines from northern Portugal were shipped out on the Atlantic Ocean. These wines were very welcome because the Douro wines proved to be of a superior quality.

In the intervening time, the British had been importing French wines, notably a wine they called 'claret' from Bordeaux. But then another war with France that began in 1689 effectively shut off their supply of French wine. The English and Scottish merchants that were in Portugal had anticipated this conflict, sending Douro wines to Britain where they were more favourably received than the thin and harsh wines that had arrived from Portugal in earlier times.

Many of the earliest 'port houses' (port producers and shippers) date from the late 1600s and early 1700s, and are still in business today. The oldest is C. N. Kopke & Ca Lda, a German company established in Portugal in 1638. The oldest British firms are Warre's, which was established in 1670; Croft, which was established by two partners in 1678; and Quarles Harris, dating from 1680, when a partner in the firm arrived in Oporto. These companies were among the very first to ship wine called simply *vinho do Porto* (wine from Porto) out to the rest of the world. The Treaty of Methuen in 1703 codified a favoured-nation status for Portugal's wines being exported to England, and at this point in history, the British were very glad to have this improved 'port wine'.

Improvements had definitely been made. It is recorded that a couple of wine merchants first made the hazardous and extremely uncomfortable journey up from Porto to the Douro River vineyards in 1678. Near the Douro, they stopped at a monastery in Lamego, where they saw the abbot adding some distilled spirit (unaged brandy) to the monastery's wine while it was still fermenting. Adding spirits at this point kills the yeast before it can consume all the sugar in the grape juice and ferment the juice into alcohol. The resultant wine is sweet, to a greater or lesser degree. After fortification (the addition of spirits), the finished wine is also higher in alcohol. Fortifying the wine seemed to make the wine more robust and better able both to age well and to withstand the rigours of shipping. This technique was also being used in other winemaking areas, notably to the north, in France's Armagnac and Cognac regions. But the fortification of port wine wasn't ubiquitous in the seventeenth and eighteenth centuries, especially in great vintages when the wine was strong and sweet on its own.

The autocratic Marquis de Pombal, who – in addition to serving as a top government official – was instrumental in fortified wine development in Portugal in the 18th century, both in the Douro Valley and in Lisbon.

Port wines grew in quality and importance over the next few centuries, though not without some setbacks due to political conflicts as well as regulatory and other issues. Sometimes there was a scarcity of wine. At other times there was an over-abundance due to a variety of factors, from merchants warehousing the wines to create scarcity, to producers adulterating the wines to add volume. In the latter case, seizing the opportunity of an increased demand for port wines, some port suppliers adulterated their ports with everything from harsh, Spanish red wine to large quantities of dried elderberries in order to amplify the volume and boost the intensity of colour and flavour in their 'port wine' to maximize profits. At times, both sugar and sweet wine made from raisins were added to some wines in order to mimic the flavours of port.

The overproduction of inferior port eventually caused a collapse in the industry in the mid-1700s. Order in the port sector was imposed by the famous Marquis de Pombal who presided over a general 'reign of terror' as a self-appointed representative of the relatively weak King José I, from 1755 to 1777. Pombal imposed strict quality and quantity measures on all aspects of port wine production, not all of which were received well – especially because during that era the British shippers were discriminated against. Pombal wanted to make the port industry more Portuguese, so he appointed local tax collectors, who somehow built themselves fabulous mansions, a few of which are still dotted around the countryside today.

However, the marquis did help the port industry in the long run, in some ways. One positive result of Pombal's decrees was the demarcation of the port-producing regions by quality in 1756, a system that endures to this day. He also required strict punishment for any wine adulteration, and his rules have helped maintain the high standards of port production over the centuries.

Fortunately for the British, the growers and other factions of the industry that were discriminated against, Pombal's rule lasted only a little more than twenty years. During that time, port exports increased in quality and in volume, and the British merchants were able to take advantage of this when they got back into the game.

From the beginning in the late 1600s, it had been the custom for British merchant families in the port industry to send a member of the family (and his wife and children) to live in Porto, in a rarefied atmosphere where all social interaction was conducted among British families. Young boys were sent back to England for school and to find British wives. Girls were expected to marry British men. It's only in the past couple of decades that this archaic custom began to change. Once it began, it moved fast. At the end of the twentieth century it was merely 'acceptable' to the British in Portugal to social-

Each port bottle could have its own style when glass was hand-blown, as in this historical bottle from the Taylor-Fladgate collection.

ize and intermarry with the Portuguese; now it is normal. However, whether Portuguese or British, there are hardly any women in the port industry; it is still a man's world.

Throughout most of port's history, the ship-pers did not own vineyards. An exception is one of the oldest existing port houses, popularly known as Taylor-Fladgate, which purchased its first vineyards in 1744. Taylor-Fladgate was established in 1692 and has remained a leader in the port world into the twenty-first century. (It is now officially part of the company called the Fladgate Partnership, and also holds the honour of a Royal Warrant for supplying port by appointment to Her Majesty Queen Elizabeth II.)

The term 'port shipper' and 'port house' are used interchangeably here – and the meaning

Historical hand-blown port bottle embossed with the Taylor-Fladgate logo.

also overlaps with 'port producer'. The first port companies were port shippers. Being responsible for getting port out of Portugal – mainly to Britain – meant that they had to ferret out port wine makers in the Douro Region, acquire the port and put it into barrels, and send it on the dangerous journey downriver to Vila Nova de Gaia to be exported. The shippers themselves would have to spend weeks making the extremely difficult trip from Porto and Gaia over the mountains and into the Douro vineyards, by foot, horse and/ or donkey. At first, port was most often shipped out in barrels and bottled on arrival. Soon, the shippers became winemakers as well as port producers: ageing the ports, then shipping and/or bottling them.

In the mid-1700s port wine was shipped out in increasing quantities, in large barrels. At that time glass bottles were used mainly as useful containers to serve the wine from the barrels. The bottles were fairly squat, and with their narrow, short necks they could sit on the table in relative safety, assuring that nothing would accidentally fall into the port. Gradually, as glass-making became more refined, port producers began to use longer, narrower bottles. The convention of

using 750 ml bottles developed serendipitously, according to Adrian
Bridge of the Fladgate Partnership. The size of the bottle equates to
the lung capacity of the glass-blowers. When moulds were first used
for bottles, this was the amount of air a given blower could infuse
into his mould in one large breath. Later, by around 1810, the size
of the bottle was standardized.

With cork being native to Portugal, producers learned how to
stop up the bottles in a manner that allowed the hearty, rustic wine
to age into a smoother, more complex and much more pleasurable
beverage. At first, bottles were used only for the best vintages of port.
Two of the first great bottled vintages recorded are 1765 and 1775.
The early vintage ports were not aged for very long, probably up to
five or ten years. They might have had less amplitude of flavour if
they were first aged in barrels (which oxidized the wine) and then
bottled later. Catalogues of the time indicate barrel ageing
of three to five years, much like the late bottled vintage
ports or tawny colheitas of today.

Port shippers acquired grapes and wine, and were
responsible for blending and ageing as well as transportation, which tied up quite a bit of capital, a situation
which the British merchants and traders were trained to
handle. During the latter part of the eighteenth century
and through the nineteenth, the port industry continued
to expand, with some inventions, and some setbacks, too.

Port shipments continued to grow and port's status also
continued to escalate. By the mid-nineteenth century fortification had become a standard process in port production.
Originally, port wine's inherent sweetness played into the
class structure of England, when it was an indication of
superiority to be able to afford sugar and other sweetened
foods and drinks. (In addition, humans are hardwired to
like sweet flavours.)

During the nineteenth century, the custom of drinking
port belonged to the nobility and high society in Britain,

Though the capacity
of the port bottle was
standardized, the
exact form of the bottle
continued to evolve, as
shown by this bottle
from 1900.

Nineteenth-century coloured lithograph of the cities of Oporto and Vila Nova de Gaia, facing each other across the busy Douro River near the Atlantic Coast.

many of whom apparently drank to excess. Stories are told of gentlemen falling off their horses and dying while riding home drunk from dinner parties. Perhaps that is when their wives stepped in and began the custom of 'withdrawing' from the dining room to wait for their husbands to complete their end-of-dinner port ritual. The men would then join the women in the drawing room where they were sipping tea and perhaps liqueurs, so they could proceed home together, safely tucked into their carriages with a servant to drive them.

At this time war and other conflicts also inundated the port world. The French invaded Portugal in the Napoleonic Wars of the early 1800s. While defending the land, the British hero the Duke of Wellington and his officers were well supplied with port during their fight against the French. Following that, there was a period of unrest in Portugal that lasted until 1834 when peace was established, along with a constitutional monarchy; Maria II ascended to the throne at the age of fifteen, after her father Pedro IV died that year.

This is not to say that everything went smoothly from the mid-nineteenth century on. Towards the end of the century Portugal's grapes began to fall victim to the same two plagues that gripped the rest of the European grapes: oidium and then phylloxera. Phylloxera essentially killed all the wine grapevines (*Vitis vinifera*) in Europe, and the only solution was to replant every vineyard with *Vitis vinifera* vines grafted onto American (non-*Vinifera*) rootstock that was resistant to phylloxera, a process that continues to this day.

Phylloxera invaded Portugal fairly early, in 1868, and once a solution to the problem was discovered, the Portuguese wine industry was one of the first to recover, while the epidemic ravaged northern French vineyards into the twentieth century. The port industry continued to thrive until the First World War put a dampener on exports. Unrest in the Portuguese government, Prohibition in the u.s., a worldwide depression and then the Second World War further disheartened the port industry. Instead of recovering after the war, the port industry faced competition from other wines from all over Europe, as soldiers returned home with tastes for wine from other countries. After that, when workers around the world began to get paid holidays, even lower- and middle-class people could afford the time and money to broaden their horizons with travel, foods and wines from other lands.

In addition, Portugal was ruled by a dictatorship from 1926 to 1974, and was culturally and politically cut off from the rest of the world. While the economies of Europe and the u.s. rebounded exuberantly after the Second World War, Portugal's did not. Portugal fell under a depression in the 1940s and '50s, and with few prospects for making a living in the countryside, the rural population of Portugal decamped for the cities. Many left Portugal altogether, so it was difficult for port shippers to find workers for their vineyards and wineries. At that time, Portuguese colonies were also fighting for their own independence, which created further unrest, financial drain and cultural conflicts.

Over the past 250 years, fortunes have been won and lost, families have bought and sold port houses, and more recently multinational corporations have entered and exited the business of port. But the big names still remain the top-quality port producers – important names to know include Cockburn, Croft, Delaforce, Dow, Ferreira, Fladgate, Fonseca, Graham, Harvey's, Offley, Real Comanhis Velha, Sandeman, Symington and Taylor. They are the family names of port shippers who have been involved for hundreds of years. A significant proportion of these names are still British.

The Douro Vineyard Area

Though the distance from Porto to the vineyards of the Douro River Valley is only around 120 km (75 mi.), before modern transportation this was a nearly insurmountable journey through mountainous terrain. With the current motorway it's an hour-and-a-half's drive. On the train, it's about two hours. But until the railway was built in the late 1800s, it took several days of traversing wild, forested hills to reach Peso da Régua (generally known simply as 'Régua'), which is the first major town in the Douro – and additional days to reach the eastern Douro villages and *quintas* with their vineyards.

Now there are day-long port wine cruises along the Douro River for sightseers. Locks and dams on the Douro enable small cruise ships to glide serenely along the river as tourists gaze up at the steep, terraced vineyards while snapping photographs and sipping port – oblivious of the historical dangers undergone by the port producers for nearly three hundred years.

Until motorways were built along the Douro in the mid-twentieth century, it took several death-defying days to ship heavy, wooden casks of port to the port lodges of Gaia on small, open *barco rabelo* boats over perilous rapids. Some of the producers did not defy death: they drowned. One of the most prominent people in port's history lost his life here in the Valeira Rapids in 1761. He was an Englishman named Joseph John Forrester who was the first to make a detailed map of the port vineyards and the Douro Region, and whose cartographic details remain important to this day. Legend has it that he was keeping company with Dona Antonia Adelaide Ferreira, who was considered a visionary in the port industry. She had been married to the owner of Quinta Vesuvio until he died in 1744. She then married her vineyard manager, probably for the sake of propriety because it was important for a woman to be married. Dona Ferreira was a very savvy businesswoman who acquired many vineyards and estates and produced impressive amounts of port under the Ferreira name. Ferreira and her Quinta Vesuvio are still important names in port today.

Forrester was Dona Ferreira's companion until he drowned off of a boat traversing the tempestuous Douro River. Visitors to Quinta do Vesuvio are told that this tragedy occurred because Forrester was gallantly carrying a heavy money belt for Dona Ferreira. The ladies

Before motorways were built, port was transported by river from the vineyards. The barrels – and people – all took the dangerous journey down the Douro River, loaded onto small *barco rabelo* boats like this one from Graham's Quinta dos Malvedos, in 1955.

The Symington Family Estate's present-day Quinta do Vesuvio with its vineyards following the undulating curves of the Douro River.

on the boat were supposedly saved because their crinolines and skirts filled with air, so they floated on the water. Years later, Forrester's son allegedly heard of the deathbed confession of a peasant who had robbed Forrester's corpse when it washed ashore on the river. In any case, the money was never found.

Many people working in the vineyards and living in the area also drowned when the Douro River flooded; it was considered very dangerous until the completion of one of the largest dams in the world in 1963, on the border of Portugal and Spain. (Coincidentally, 1963 was also the year of one of the top vintages of port ever.) The site of the Aldeadávila Dam is in Spain, a location strongly resented by the Portuguese for some time: they felt victimized because Spain's use of the dam's overflow capacity often caused perilously uneven currents and levels in the Douro, either flooding the railway and lanes along the region or leaving them high and dry.

Many roads in the Douro region were built high above the river and the vineyards, along the tops of the hills. And there aren't many bridges at all along the 80 km (50 mi.) of the Douro. So if a producer or worker wanted to go to his home along the river or visit someone across the river, they used the simplest method: a boat – which would be impossible if the river's situation was not stable. Eventually more dams and locks were built downstream in Portugal, which then made it easier to stabilize this section of the Douro.

Though the Douro is the main waterway along which the port vineyards are visible today, there is another important river here, the Corgo, which flows south into the Douro, and which also has wonderful vistas of terraced vineyards on the precipitous hills above the river. The Corgo is not the only Douro tributary in the wine region, but early on it became the most well-known, very possibly because it is the furthest west and thus was the first that travellers from Porto encountered after crossing the Marão hills. In addition, it is on the north side of the Douro, which was the first bank to be cultivated, so vineyards could face south. In the eighteenth century, the southern banks of the Douro and the eastern lands extending to the border of Spain were savage lands full of menacing animals such as wolves and exceptionally fierce wild pigs.

Also, the Douro was only navigable up to the Valeira Rapids until the large granite rock that nearly blocked the river was removed in 1791. After that, the Douro vineyards began to expand east, and today the official demarcated region extends for about 250,000 hectares (over 600,000 acres), from the Marão mountains to the Spanish border. Vineyards are now planted on about 18 per cent of the total area, on both sides of the Douro River and its tributaries.

Grapes

According to the Port and Douro Wines Institute (IVDP), the grapes for port wine must be grown within the demarcated Douro region of northern Portugal, and the wine must be made only from certain specified grapes native to the region. In the past there were around fifty different grapes grown in this area. For centuries, the farmers

hedged their bets by growing many different g
variety did not do well in a particular year. Nov
understanding of viticulture, soils and microclim
has dwindled to about thirty varieties.

Port is made mainly from red grapes, the most well known being Tinta Roriz (known elsewhere as Tempranillo) along with Touriga Nacional, Tinto Cão, Touriga Francisca and Tinta Barroca. In fact, consumers have become so caught up in the New World phenomenon of labelling a wine by its grape(s) that there is some danger that port wines will be made with fewer and fewer grape varieties in order to specify them on the label, so that they will become familiar to consumers. If so, this will threaten not only the complexity of the wines but the celebrated historical diversity of the vineyards.

Today, the main, officially sanctioned white grapes are, in alphabetical order: Arinto, Boal, Cercial, Côdega, Esgana Cão, Donzelhino Branco, Folgasão, Gouveio, Malvasia Corada, Malvasia Fina, Moscatel Galego, Rabigato, Samarrinho and Viosinho. The major red grapes are Bastardo, Cornifesto, Donzelhino, Malvasia, Mourisco Tinto, Periquita, Rufete, Tinta Amarela, Tinta Barca, Tinta Barroca, Tinta Francisca, Tinta Roriz, Tinta Cão, Touriga Francisca and Touriga Nacional.

At this point it's a good idea to go through the delicate process of port wine production, from winemaking to fortification. As mentioned earlier, 'fortification' simply refers to the addition of a neutral spirit, like an unaged brandy, to 'fortify' or strengthen the wine. This process was used from the Middle Ages on for wine that was going to be shipped a long way. It had the added effect of creating a wine that would also age much longer. Though fortification had been used in making some ports since the late 1600s, the process was not standardized then.

The wine was fermented 'dry' – and could have been a different 'dryness' each year, depending on the date of harvest, how much fruit sugar the grapes contained and the fermentation process.

Natural yeasts cannot live in an environment (a wine) that has too high an alcohol content, and different yeasts have different tolerances. Basically, yeast is responsible for wine fermentation by consuming grape sugar and converting it into alcohol (with some other by-products like CO_2). If a type of yeast doesn't do well in an environment of, say, over 10 per cent alcohol, it will die off, and the resultant wine will be a little sweeter than if the yeast had been able to live and keep converting the sugars in a wine up to 11 or 12 per cent alcohol.

Port is a wine, and as such it is made the same way all wines are made: by fermenting juice extracted from wine grapes, *Vitis vinifera*, of various varieties. But the method of extracting the juice and the colour is a little different. In a technique probably used since Roman times, the harvested grapes have traditionally been put into square or rectangular wide stone basins called *lagares* which are several metres wide, and about 1 metre (3 ft) deep. Grape treaders in shorts climb into the *lagares* and work in lines across and back, in both directions. They do this for several hours at a time, several days in a row – sometimes singing, to keep the beat.

It was customary for this to be done only by men, as women were thought to be 'unclean' at certain times of the month. It is only in recent decades that foot treading the grapes has been replaced – though not completely – with machines. The treading machines were not simple to develop; it took several port houses numerous trials and many years to duplicate the foot-action of humans. Some port producers still insist on foot treading, for a number of reasons including the quality of the finished port, the maintenance of the tradition, the marketing value of the photos of happy foot treaders – or a combination of all three. Even these port producers, though, use machines to de-stem the bunches of grapes first.

Why didn't they change their methods earlier? In the twenty-first century it might seem odd that port production only recently started to use mechanization. However, electricity did not reliably run throughout the Douro Valley until the 1960s, many decades after it was commonly used in cities and towns in much of the world. Then there's also the 'If it's not broken, don't fix it' mentality, meaning that port was selling well when it was made in the traditional, non-industrialized manner.

Port Styles

Port is actually made in only two major styles. The different styles of the final product derive from the fact that port can be either 'bottle-aged' or 'wood-aged' (in barrels). The finished wines turn out quite differently in colour, aroma and flavour. Also, there are several different styles of both bottle-aged and barrel-aged ports. Many wine drinkers believe that the best wines are aged in barrels, but that's not always the case. The renowned vintage ports are always bottle-aged.

Port is one of the most complicated of fortified wines, so it's worth looking at all the different types of port to gain an understanding of how the styles are produced, aged and served – whether the serving is as an aperitif wine, in a cocktail or as an after-dinner drink. All three of these occasions can demand different port styles. One thing they have in common: all ports, except vintage ports, are made to be consumed as soon as they are purchased. Only vintage ports are made to improve with age in the bottle.

Bottle-aged Ports

The most celebrated port wine is vintage port. It is a bottle-aged port, which might seem counterintuitive to consumers conditioned to believe that barrel-ageing is a requirement for fine winemaking. Vintage port has long been considered the finest expression of port. Each producer makes it only a few times in a decade, when the harvests are outstanding in quality and balance.

Vintage port is an exceptionally complex and full wine, made to be enjoyed for decades. Notes of red fruits, dark-red berries, plum and cocoa permeate this wine; it also has a great acidity which balances the wine and modifies the perception of sweetness. It must be 'declared' a vintage eighteen months after harvest and must be bottled between the second half of the second year after harvest and the end of the third year after harvest. After that, vintage ports are not released (available for purchase) until they have settled for some time after bottling. But at that point they are years or even decades from their optimal level of quality, so there is no need to rush to purchase – unless one is concerned about shortages of availability, which is what wine merchants will caution consumers about.

Traditionally, vintage ports were considered mature enough to drink only about twenty years after harvest. A practice developed among the British upper classes of 'laying down a pipe of port' when their sons or godsons were born. The port would then be opened and served at the boys' twenty-first birthdays, which are customarily a major celebration in Britain. Originally, a 'pipe' was a long wooden barrel that held 534 litres of port, the equivalent of about 720 bottles, which is sixty cases of today's 750 ml bottles. Nowadays a pipe has been standardized to a volume of 550 litres – more than enough for a party.

In recent years the ageing requirement for vintage port has been shortened to closer to ten years because of improvements in grape-growing, winemaking and ageing methods. It's not necessary to start drinking a vintage port after ten years, though; it may be more enjoyable to wait the full twenty years. And there is no need to rush even then, because vintage ports will be at their peak for drinking up to forty years after harvest; many vintage ports can also last much longer. A substantial percentage of vintage ports have proven to offer wonderful flavours and aromas for sixty, seventy or even eighty years – which is quite a thrill to drink!

More recently, another style of vintage port has gained popularity in this category: single-quinta vintage port. This port is made from grapes grown on one single estate (*quinta*) in one particular year.

Pleasingly rounded, hand-blown, historical bottle for port.

This happens in a harvest when the producer feels that one particular section of an estate's vineyards is producing optimal-quality wines in a year that is not generally considered 'vintage' quality in the whole port region. In other words, only one segment of an estate has produced superb grapes that can turn into a superior wine for that year.

Wood-aged Port

Several styles of ports are aged in barrels and some in larger vats. Because these barrels and vats are made of wood, these ports are referred to as 'wood aged'. Both ruby and late bottled vintage (LBV) ports are aged in large vats, but for a relatively short time, thus preserving the colour and fruit in the wine.

The first (entry-level) tier of wood-aged port is very dark red in colour; it is fruity, strong and sweet, with great richness and appeal. Young port wines made in this style are named after their colour in the bottle: ruby red. There is also a ruby reserva tier of wines, made with specially selected grapes. Both of these are at the lower end of port pricing. Ruby reserva falls in between a ruby and an LBV port in style and price.

LBV port is made with ruby reserva-quality grapes but in a vintage style. LBVs are made with grapes from a single vintage, and bottled after four to six years of wood ageing; they are meant to be a kind of 'introduction' to the vintage style of port, but at a lower price. LBV port does not need further ageing; it is ready to be consumed when it is released on the market. The wines are also red, but not as deep a colour as ruby ports.

Tawny Port

Tawny ports are named after the finished colour of the wine. They are aged in wooden barrels, which are called casks in the port trade. Though tawnies are made with red grapes, this type of wood-ageing softens the wine, gives it a brown-toned colour and adds more complexity during its development. Both the wood of the cask and some resultant interaction with oxygen create finished tawny ports that range in colour from tan to deep amber, depending on the age of the wine.

Young tawny ports are aged in seasoned oak barrels for at least three years. They are handled so they gain no other organoleptic elements (aromas or flavours) from the wood. They are lighter in style and less fruity than the bottle-aged ports; their aromas and flavours contain elements of baking spices and dried fruits and nuts. Tawny reserva ports are similar in style, but are blends of wines aged longer, for five to seven years.

Older tawnies are designed to be bottled according to how many decades they have been aged, and this is indicated on the labels. The wines are specially created to be aged for either ten, twenty, thirty or forty years. Ten-year tawny port is a more defined, more mature version of tawny reserva. Twenty-year tawny is aged in smaller oak casks, which give the wine more wood-aged characteristics such as toasted hints of vanilla and dried fruits. The thirty-year tawnies are more complex, and their barrel-ageing has begun to show in some oxidation in the flavours and aromas. The oldest year-designated tawnies are the forty-years, which have more concentrated flavours and more oak influence; they are at their peak of complexity.

There is one more style of tawny port: colheita (pronounced *kohl-YAY-tah*). A colheita is a tawny port wine made with grapes from a single vintage and aged in oak for at least seven years. Colour may vary from gold to reddish to pale brown, and the aromas and flavours are also variable depending on age – and on the particular vintage, of course.

Crusted Port

Crusted port is a category of its own, one that UK consumers might be more familiar with because it is rarely seen in the U.S. It is wood-aged for three to four years, then bottled. It is specially made to 'throw a crust' when mature, which means there is some sediment left in the bottle. The interaction of the wine with this particular sediment enriches the wine, adding a measure of complexity.

White and Rosé Ports

White and rosé ports are considered more casual, and somewhat more modern. A chilled white port is a delightful aperitif on a hot day. Though the French discovered this early on, the U.S. and UK have just started catching on. But in Portugal many port producers seem slightly embarrassed by the existence of white port; they may drink it but they haven't really wanted to talk about it – until recently, when the popularity of the drink overcame their reticence. Most white port is sweet, but in fact it can be made with varying levels of sweetness in different categories: extra seco, seco, doce and lagrima. There is even a rare, reserva level of white port that is aged in wood for a minimum of seven years, until it darkens to a golden yellow.

Rosé is the newest style of port, produced and exported for the international rosé craze of the early twenty-first century. It is made with red grapes, and it is considered a fun beverage today.

Because of the popularity of sparkling wines, some port producers are even starting to make sparkling port-style wines. This is not a category currently sanctioned by the governing body of port, the IVDP – though perhaps this is something they will consider in the future.

Declaring a Vintage

For a vintage to be 'declared', generally all the major port houses will agree that a particular harvest was of exceptional quality. Unanimity is not a requirement but a vintage declaration must be sanctioned by the IVDP. If a particular port producer does not feel its ports are of vintage quality, it is not required to participate.

Conversely, if a producer feels that its ports are of the highest quality, this producer may make some vintage port, as long as the IVDP deems it to be of high enough quality. There may be extenuating circumstances, including anything from vineyard location and micro-climate to a significant anniversary for the producer. In this case, the producer may produce a very small amount of vintage port from only some of its vineyards.

There are no minimum quantities required for a vintage port production, but there are maximums, which are computed as a percentage of total port production. Quantities are kept under strict control in order to maintain quality and limit overproduction; it can be tempting for producers to make as much of the high-prestige, higher-priced vintage port as possible.

As previously mentioned, vintage port quality harvests tend to occur several times a decade, roughly every three or four years, though they can occur in consecutive years. Because vintages are not declared until six months after the following harvest, port producers are also able to make marketing a consideration in their vintage declarations, having also been through the following harvest, too. Even though a vintage port is made to be consumed ten or twenty years afterwards, just a few months after a harvest, experienced winemakers would have a good enough idea of how a vintage will turn out to make the call.

The amount of all port is strictly regulated in a system known as *beneficio*. The IVDP defines *beneficio* as 'the Portuguese expression used to describe the adding of grape brandy to fermenting wine' but in reality this word has come to describe the whole process of authorizing the amount of grape juice that each producer can legally make into port in a given year, based on factors such as the classification of vineyards (A to F) and the quantity of port needed for the marketplace.

Since Portugal joined the European Union in 1986, many port producers have been much happier about the quality of the spirit they can access for fortifying the wine – a spirit that also must be approved by the IVDP. Formerly, much of the Portuguese-produced spirit they were allowed to use was not of great quality; now they can access spirit from whatever other EU countries they prefer – usually France or Spain, these days. This is extremely important because the fortifying spirit makes up 20 per cent of the finished port.

Serving Port

After all these descriptions of different styles of port, it would be helpful to understand how to serve them and when to drink them.

In terms of whether to wait or consume a port after purchase, the answer is simple: drink everything but vintage port right away, within a year or two. Except for vintage ports, they are made to be enjoyed as soon as you acquire them; they are not made to improve in the bottle, and their quality may even degrade after a few years.

As mentioned before, vintage ports are crafted to be consumed ten, twenty or more years after the harvest (vintage) date on the bottle. However, once a bottle of vintage port is opened, it's best to finish it that day. These bottle-aged ports do not hold up as long as other styles once opened. Other ports, after opening, should be kept chilled in a wine fridge or even a regular refrigerator. They should not be left at room temperature. LBV ports and crusted ports should be consumed within four or five days. Ruby and ruby reserva wines will last for up to ten days; tawny and tawny reserva ports will hold up for three or four weeks. Aged tawnies (ten, twenty, thirty and forty years) and older colheitas will last for at least a month, and sometimes up to four months if they are kept chilled – as will the very rare, aged white ports.

Standard white ports as well as ruby and rosé ports are at their best when consumed within eight or ten days after opening the bottle – consumed chilled, of course. In fact, rosé ports are made to be sipped well-chilled, at around 4°C (40°F), while white ports can be served a bit warmer at 8–10°C (45–50°F). Ruby ports are best at 12–16°C (55–60°F). Keep tawnies a bit cooler at 10–14°C (50–57°F). For vintage ports, keep them cooler than modern room temperature, ideally serving them at 15–18°C (60–65°F).

The simple solution for serving port is to use a white wine glass, or any smallish wine glass of good quality. The IVDP has an approved port glass, and there are some other high-end lines of glassware with their own glasses recommended for port. These are all typically stemmed glasses, with an elongated (tall) bowl. The glass itself is shorter than a white wine glass, being about 15 cm (6 in.) high. The top of the bowl is a bit smaller than the diameter of the bowl, so the aromas of the port are concentrated and held in the glass. The bowl will hold a total of 190 ml (around 6.4 oz.); a typical 'pour' or serving size is 75 ml (3 oz.), which fills the glass nicely to about halfway up the bowl.

In order to serve a port correctly, it must be opened correctly, and different styles of ports have different stoppers for their bottles. Vintage ports have a traditional natural cork stopper that is opened with a corkscrew. Ideally, the bottle will not need to be re-stoppered because it should be consumed when it is opened. Other styles of ports are easier to open and reclose because they have a flat, plastic cap attached to their natural cork stoppers. The stopper is further sealed against air with a synthetic covering. After removing the covering, it is easy to twist out the cork – and to replace it after serving.

With very old ports, sometimes the corks become crumbly and/or stuck in the neck of the bottles. In that case, there is a ritual method of opening a bottle involving long, metal port tongs and a feather from a bird. The tongs are heated to red-hot at one end, then clamped onto the bottle neck for a few seconds, which creates an invisible fissure in the glass. Immediately afterward, the end of a feather is dipped in ice-cold water and then run along the fissure in the neck. (Lacking a feather, the corner of a wet cloth will do.) If all goes well, there will be an audible crack. At that point, the top of the bottle's neck – cork, seal and all – can be broken off by hand. Of course, it's necessary to use a fine mesh strainer when decanting the port to eliminate any sediment or tiny shards of glass.

Decanting in general is often recommended before serving older or crusted ports. Before opening, though, the bottle should be taken from its horizontal storage and set upright in a cool place for a day or so, if possible.

There's another port ritual that involves decanting, especially older vintages. The bottle is positioned in front of a lighted

Vintage ports are usually poured into decanters shortly before serving, to avoid the sediment that languishes in the bottoms of the port bottles; it is a delicate operation requiring a steady hand.

candle in a candle holder. The bottle is gently tilted so the port runs slowly into the decanter. The candle's flame stays in position behind the bottle so the person decanting the port can see through the bottle and stop pouring out the wine before any sediment in the bottle comes out. Often the wine is also poured through a fine mesh sieve positioned above the mouth of the decanter to catch any sediment poured by accident.

In the heyday of port consumption in Britain – during the nineteenth and much of the twentieth century – it was customary to decant the port and continuously pass the decanter around the table, always to the left. It's not hard to imagine that after a while, a person might become so involved in the conversation at the table that he – it's always 'he', because women didn't drink after-dinner port with the men – would forget to pass the port.

Two very polite methods evolved for dealing with this. One is in the form of a question. A dinner companion waiting too long for the port decanter could turn to the person on his right and ask: 'Do you know the Bishop of Norwich?' The Bishop of Norwich is a real member of the Church of England, but a given person at a dinner party would not be expected to know him.

So the answer would be, 'No I don't know the Bishop; why do you ask?'

The first person would reply, 'Well, he's notoriously stingy about passing the port.' Presumably this would get the point across, and the port would be passed along right away. In the highest social circles, every so often the person would actually be acquainted with the bishop, which would only create further confusion.

The second method of ensuring the port is passed is a little more devious – or clever, depending on one's point of view. The port would be served in a hoggit – a decanter with a rounded bottom – so that the decanter could never be set down on the table; it had to be continuously passed along. This technique was for serious imbibers only!

Cocktails

In the nineteenth century, and through the first half of the twentieth, vodka and gin were not nearly as popular – or obtainable – as they are now. For cocktails, bartenders would use the readily available spirits and fortified wines of the day, such as brandy, port and sherry. Many popular early punches had a base of port wine.

Today, the simplest port cocktail is called Port Tonic, which is literally port on ice, topped with a tonic mixer. Traditionally this was made with white port, though it works nicely with ruby port, too.

Bartenders in major cities around the globe have been inspired to use all types of port in their classic, signature and new cocktails. It is now possible to find a port cocktail in every mode from sparkling styles to classic Sours, from Martinis to dessert drinks, in all the finest bars and restaurants. Bartenders are now publishing the recipes for their best port cocktails each season – and motivating home mixologists to participate in this revival.

The Landscape of the Port World Today

Recent changes in port production have been made possible by modernizations as simple as electricity, mechanization and transportation improvements in the last few decades. Add in oenology and viticulture research, and great advances have become possible. But it's not automatic. Because port is a highly regulated industry, every alteration in the status quo has to be approved by the governing body, the IVDP (which has undergone several iterations; this is the current name). And because of its many centuries of tradition, the benefit of every adjustment has to be rigorously proved to the members who are part of this association.

Traditionally, port houses would try not to declare consecutive vintages. It is relatively rare that stellar vintages occur one after the other, but it has happened about 25 per cent of the time in the past 260 years. Consecutive declaration affects market value; it's harder

The original port cocktail: Port Tonic, made with dry white port and tonic water, served over ice with optional garnishes such as fresh lime or mint leaves.

to promote a vintage port if there has just been a vintage declared the year before.

Recently there have been indications of some push-back to this custom. In the past few years, it seems at least one port house (not the same one every year) has been declaring a small amount of vintage port every year. This follows the trend towards single-quinta colheitas and ports – and the global proliferation of single-vineyard wines in general. If a port producer has a defined area that produces enough exceptional wine in any given year, in theory there's no reason why it can't submit this to the IVDP to approve its vintage quality. If it becomes common, this would turn the vintage port convention on its ear – but it could also help by making vintage port consistently available to consumers, much as all fine wines have new vintages of their wines available every year. Though this phenomenon flies in the face of convention, it could be a welcome change for the recently declining vintage port market.

Looking at the physical landscape, the port wine region is currently divided into three areas: Baixa Corgo ('lower Corgo' which is west of the Corgo River and has 18 per cent under vine), Cima Corgo ('upper Corgo' east of the Corgo River, with 38 per cent under vine) and Douro Superior ('upper Douro' on both sides of the Douro River,

Classic dry-stone wall terraces in the vineyards at the Terra Feita Port quinta in Portugal's Douro Valley.

with 44 per cent under vine). The countryside around the vineyards remains fairly wild. It has little rainfall, and the hills are incredibly steep. Summer or winter, the areas around the *quintas* feel remote and inhospitable. Though the Douro runs through the middle, it literally runs by, without adding any welcoming moisture to the surrounding hills.

Yet 33,000 small farmers live or work here, each with an average small vineyard of 1 hectare (about 2.5 acres). Today, in order to make a living, farmers often live or work in the nearby cities and towns – as far away as Porto – and come out on weekends to tend to their vineyards. As they have done for hundreds of years, they work the vineyards by hand on the sheer hillsides; everything from planting to weeding to pruning to harvesting has to be done vine by vine, with back-breaking labour.

In terms of location, it's not surprising that most of the smaller farmers have plots in the western part of the region; the eastern area of the upper Douro is where the larger vineyards are, having been planted later by more prosperous families or companies. In terms of soil, most of the Douro consists of schist with some granite. When disturbed, the schist breaks up into small fragments and then into powder.

Originally, vines were planted on steep hills that were terraced with dry stone walls. This has created beautiful vistas that are becoming harder and harder to maintain because most of the stonemasons who understand the craft have died out – though some of the port producers are making the effort to maintain the stone walls. However, the overall landscape of lovely, undulating terraces along the rivers is now, as of 2001, part of a UNESCO World Heritage site. As stated by UNESCO:

The Alto Douro Region has been producing wine for nearly two
thousand years and its landscape has been moulded by human
activities . . . The components of the Alto Douro landscape
are representative of the full range of activities associated
with winemaking – terraces, quintas (wine-producing farm
complexes), villages, chapels, and roads . . . The cultural landscape
of the Alto Douro is an outstanding example of a traditional
European wine-producing region, reflecting the evolution of
this human activity over time.

In the late twentieth and early twenty-first centuries, machines
were brought in to open up new areas to plant grapevines, and to
reshape some slopes to make it possible to plant vines that could be
mechanically harvested. This entails widening the terraces for the
vines that are planted in horizontal lines, and recontouring other
areas where vines can be planted vertically as long as the gradients
of the slopes are not too great; if the hills are too steep, during heavy
rains the topsoil will be carried to the bottom of the hills – and
maybe right into the river – and there is little enough topsoil as it is.

Currently, there are three types of vineyard row plantings in the
Douro. In additional to the traditional, narrow terraces built with
dry stone walls, there are newer *patamar* terraces which are wider
and taller, constructed mainly in the 1970s and '80s. This was part
of a modernization scheme for the Douro which is now seen as only
partly successful – and not resulting in optimal quality wine. Some
of the *patamares* on hillsides with a gradient of less than 30 per cent
have gradually been replaced with the new vertical rows of vines,
without terracing. This perpendicular arrangement is called *vinha
ao alto*. Other *patamares* are being replaced with newly engineered
terraces of a different size that have been developed to be more
appropriate to today's sustainable agricultural practices.

Only gradually did port producers come to the realization that
the world had changed around them, and they had to institute their
own advancements in promotion as well as in the vineyards and

Spring green bursts out along the classic terraced vineyards at Warre's Quinta do Retiro in the Douro Valley.

wineries in the mid-twentieth century. They also began to actively market their ports. But at that time, certain segments of the population considered advertising and marketing as a negative; the upper classes thought it was 'common' and indicated an attempt to compensate for lack of quality. However, some port producers realized they had to broaden their potential customer base and they stuck to their guns. Luckily, the 1963 vintage was one of the great vintages of the century, which provided port with more ammunition for their positive image-making.

Still, that was relatively short-lived. The social changes in the Western world that began in the 1960s meant that the custom of port as an after-dinner ritual was no longer viable. Potential port consumers usually had to drive themselves home after dinner, so evenings became a lot less likely to finish with post-prandial drinks, except on the most special occasions. In addition, the commercial export of ports had been interrupted too many times in the twentieth century owing to external wars, internal unrest in Portugal and other factors.

Other changes were taking place within the port industry, such as the issue of bottling. At the end of the Second World War, only about 2 per cent of port was bottled in Porto. When the producers of vintage port, which had mainly been shipped in casks, began to work on improving their product's image, they recognized the authenticity and authority that had always been embedded in the appeal of this wine. So more and more producers began to bottle their vintage ports in Portugal. This precipitated a change in bottling law, and all vintage ports declared after 1973 were required to be bottled in Portugal. In fact, all port wines must now be bottled in Portugal.

The old order was dead. And this is the concern that port producers have been struggling with ever since. They have just recently begun to win some battles, partly by marketing not only their ports but the majestic landscape of the Douro Valley as a destination. They have been creating new products (such as rosé and sparkling port-style wines). And they have begun appealing to modern mixologists' quests to re-create traditional cocktails, many of which were port-based drinks, since the mixology craze began in the early 2000s.

At first many port producers, with their lengthy, traditional heritage, were loath to look towards cocktails as a way to increase their sales. Having existed in a rarefied social world for so many centuries, some thought it would be demeaning to chase after the cocktail crowd. But there were a few forward thinkers like George Sandeman, who greeted the mixologists and cocktail consumers with genuine curiosity and enthusiasm – and they have embraced him back with equal fervour. Sandeman is one of the oldest names in port, having been founded in 1780. The company itself is now part of the large Portuguese wine conglomerate Sogrape. However, Sogrape has been wise enough to step back and let the well-known Sandeman name take centre stage – along with George himself, a very tall man who projects a persona that is somehow affable, aristocratic and approachable all at the same time.

The charming Symington family, however, has always concentrated on port's historical legacy, and it is heartening to see the way that they have re-energized to accomplish this. Currently run by the fourth generation of Symingtons, in recent decades the company has essentially been admiring, acquiring and restoring the lustre of many classic port brands. The Symingtons have had a long history of involvement with the port trade, originating with an ancestor called Walter Maynard who not only became an early port shipper in 1652 (reportedly the second oldest on record), but was appointed British Consul in Porto in 1659. Jumping to 1905, the founder of the eponymous Symington dynasty, Andrew James Symington, became a partner at Warre's, the oldest port shipper, which originated in 1770. In 1912 Symington also became a partner at Dow's, which had been founded in 1798 under the original name of Silva & Cosens; his descendants became the sole owners in the 1960s.

The Symington family's modern passion for acquisition started when Graham's, founded in 1820, was put up for sale in 1970; it was acquired by Andrew James Symington's grandsons. The classic shipper Cockburn's, founded in 1815, was acquired by the fourth generation of the Symington family in 2010. In 2014 the first of the fifth generation, Charlotte Symington, entered the company – a very modern statement in an industry that has been publicly male-dominated for centuries.

Many port producers have also been modernizing their operations with another prong of port's twenty-first-century renewal: the sense of place. Only a few decades ago, the historic port lodges along the Douro in Gaia were simply warehouses. Today, they anchor a vibrant riverside lifestyle of cafes and restaurants inside the lodges, which have been expanded to include tours, tastings and museums that draw tourists from around the world.

In 2010 the Fladgate Partnership (formerly known as Taylor-Fladgate) opened the Yeatman Hotel in Gaia, thus preserving the historic Yeatman name and offering luxury accommodations across the river from Porto, within walking distance of the revitalized riverside district. Taylor's dates its origins to a first shipment of red wine in 1692 by company founder Job Bearsley. By the nineteenth century, Taylor-Fladgate had become known as Taylor, Fladgate & Yeatman after partnering with John Yeatman in 1838; the Yeatman family was instrumental in experimenting with and perfecting a variety of innovations, including new methods of grape fermentation in separate blocks. The firm itself was the first to make late bottled vintage-style ports. Through a series of mergers and acquisitions that occurred in recent decades, this company is currently composed of the illustrious port houses of Taylor, Fladgate, Yeatman, Fonseca (founded in 1815) and Croft. They are keeping the traditional names alive in port production, as well as embracing a future in the hospitality industry as tourism grows in both the city areas and vineyard regions of the Douro. The Fladgate Partnership's most recent acquisition is the historically distinguished Hotel Infante de Sagres in the centre of Porto.

In terms of general hospitality trends, tourists can now take day-long or multi-day cruises to see the historic vineyards along the Douro River. The former trading towns of Régua and Pinhão now have their own tasting centres and other activities for tourists. The Symington family, for instance, opened two visitors' centres in historic port shippers' buildings: Graham's in Gaia in 2013 and Cockburn's up in the Douro in 2015. Today, on each side of the Douro – in Porto and in Gaia – there are dozens of restaurants, cafes, port-tasting centres and modern hotels, all in wonderfully renovated centuries-old buildings spilling out onto the picturesque stone quays.

In the Douro, one of the most impressive openings is the Douro Royal Valley, a postmodern block set out in the countryside – a collection of buildings with sharp angles embodying contemporary design, including high-end spare-style guestrooms, a spa, a pool and a restaurant – a getaway where the guests never have to leave the property. Of course, there are plenty of ports to sample right on the premises.

Over at Quinta da Pacheca, in addition to sampling the wines, guests can literally sleep in barrels: barrel-shaped suites with outdoor decks set in the grounds of the winery's Wine House Hotel, across the Douro River from Régua.

In town, the Six Senses hotel provides luxurious, riverside accommodations with upscale amenities. More and more hotels are opening, taking advantage of *quintas* and other buildings that are no longer inhabited by port-related families, now that much of the business has moved to Gaia and Porto because motorways have made vineyards and wineries in the Douro more easily commutable for city-dwelling managers and employees.

3
Sherry

—◆—

Sherry has found a whole new life lately in top bars and cocktail lounges around the world. Rediscovered by wine and cocktail geeks around the turn of the twenty-first century, both dry and sweet sherries have also joined the wine lists of the most avant-garde restaurateurs. And they all stem from one small area in the south of Spain, located at the tip of the Iberian Peninsula, by the Atlantic coast. This is the same sherry which, for many wine drinkers, essentially disappeared – or at least seriously went out of fashion – towards the end of the twentieth century.

The British have been importing wines from the area around Jerez for nearly seven hundred years. For centuries sherry was served in British households in the late morning or late afternoon before lunch or dinner, or at teatime. During the latter part of the twentieth century, the prevalence of this custom, as well as the quality of the wine served, slowly waned – perhaps each of these factors influencing the other. In addition, sherry became the victim of a younger generation's rebellion against their parents in all manner of drinks, beginning in the 1970s.

Then lately, a subsequent generation seeking new, rare treasures 'discovered' sherry and began to appreciate it, to resurrect it and finally to demand – and receive – higher-quality sherries, in old and new styles, at the start of the twenty-first century. This has continued for the past couple of decades, slowly building, gradually injecting more excitement into a sherry industry that now welcomes young people's attention with open arms, and with new sherries.

Modern mixologists have found there are many advantages to including sherry wines in cocktails. Sherry flavours are tangy, sometimes salty, with the nuttiness of almonds or hazelnuts, and/or the concentrated fruit of dried apricots and raisins. A sherry can contribute several of the required component tastes of a well-balanced cocktail: fruit, acidity and depth. It can also serve as the base for a cocktail, instead of a spirit such as vodka or gin. And as a bonus, sherry-based cocktails fulfil a growing demand for lower-alcohol drinks, because sherries contain less than half the alcohol of spirits – a factor that is often appreciated now that most people must drive to and from restaurants.

Sommeliers and wine directors have also found that the lively acidity, targeted sharpness, piquant stimulation and lush evolution of different styles of dry sherries complement many types of foods. From salted nuts, olives, cheeses and smoked fish to dishes of meat and potatoes with hearty or spicy sauces, the right sherry will complement and enrich dishes in a main course. After the meal a sweet sherry can be served alongside ice cream, or paired with dessert recipes that feature nuts, dried fruits or chocolate. Sipping sherry can even be a dessert in itself.

Sherry is produced in the southern part of Spain, in three towns that comprise the 'Sherry Triangle' near the tip of the Iberian Peninsula, west of Gibraltar. The three towns are Jerez de la Frontera, Sanlúcar de Barrameda and El Puerto de Santa María. The word 'sherry' takes its name from Jerez. During the Middle Ages when the area was ruled by the Moors, the town of Jerez was called Xeres, which would have been pronounced something like 'sherrez'. In its early export days, the wine from this city was also known as 'sherris'.

Though the drier sherries are quite pale in colour, the more complex sherries and the sweeter styles are darker. However, all sherries are made only with white grapes. The finished wines range in colour from nearly clear to rich mahogany, depending on the style and age.

Only after the grapes have begun fermenting into wine do the singular processes begin that create the unique wine that is sherry. The first is fortification, which takes place at a specified point during the wine's fermentation; this is the addition of a neutral spirit, essentially an un-aged grape-based brandy. Depending on the desired style of sherry, more or less fortification will be added. Then the wines are aged in large barrels of American oak that have been 'seasoned' or prepared so that the oak wood itself does not influence the final aromas and flavours of the sherries. However, the specific amounts of oxygenation that occur inside the wooden barrels are critical to the final development of the sherry. Both the barrels and the oxygenation also contribute somewhat to the colour of the aged sherries.

The Sherry Triangle

Today, the region where sherry wines are produced is referred to in English as the Sherry Triangle, because it is composed of vineyards and production zones around three towns: Jerez, Sanlúcar de Barrameda and El Puerto de Santa María. The Spanish name for this area is the Marco de Jerez. The three Triangle towns are located in southern Spain, in the region of Andalusia, whose name reflects the many centuries of Moorish rule here, when much of Spain was known as Al-Andalus. The Moorish (Muslim) rulers were powerful in the Middle Ages. At the beginning of the eighth century they stormed in to annexe the Iberian Peninsula. They came from North

Africa, which at its closest point is a distance of only 14 kilometres (about 9 mi.) away by sea. Beginning their conquest of Iberia in AD 711, they succeeded in subjugating most of the peninsula in a relatively short time.

It wasn't until a few hundred years later that the rulers of what is now northern Spain were in a position to begin pushing back against the Moors. And it was another couple of centuries until the Aragonese and Castilians (northern Spain's Christian rulers, who each had their own domain) 'reconquered' much of the Iberian peninsula. The region now known as Andalusia was the slowest to yield to the northerners. To this day, the full name of the city of Jerez is still 'Jerez de la Frontera' because the city was located on the southern border (*frontera*) between the Christian-ruled and Muslim-ruled zones of Iberia for two hundred years, from the end of the thirteenth century to the end of the fifteenth.

King Alfonso X of Castile 'liberated' Jerez from the Moors in 1264. Because Jerez remained a border town, the king decided to distribute agricultural lands here as rewards to nobles, royal relatives, and military and church officials. The lands were needed to grow agricultural staples such as grain and grapes, so landowners would

The colours of all the different styles of sherry.

Medieval naval battle off the coast of the conflict-heavy region of Andalusia in the southern part of the Iberian Peninsula.

be able to supply both inhabitants and soldiers with food and drink. The land awards also served as incentives for those loyal to the Castilian crown to re-populate this area, which had been devastated by the fighting. According to records, one of the noble families of Jerez was an early land-grant settler: Valdespino, a great name in sherry to this day.

The Christian *Reconquista* (re-conquest) of the southern section of the Iberian Peninsula continued through the fourteenth and fifteenth centuries, until the final frontier fell to a new alliance of the Iberian ruling families of Aragon and Castile in 1492. But even before that time the wines of Jerez had become well known, and it is said that these wines helped fuel the Christian soldiers – and their horses! – in their campaigns against the Moors.

Once the Catholic Christians had retaken the land that became known as Spain, there were further terrible centuries to come, as these rulers ruthlessly captured, tortured and exiled people of other religions. But despite the fighting at the end of the Moors' occupation and the chaos of the new Castilian Inquisition, trade in coastal cities near the Strait of Gibraltar flourished during the latter half of the fifteenth century, and continued to grow during the sixteenth century. Perhaps many of the merchants were also Catholics, or perhaps this region was far enough away from the central government in Madrid for it not to matter so much. For whatever reason, the entrepreneurs who flocked to the Andalusia region included wine merchants from many lands.

At this point, the Jerez-area wines were becoming so well known and so popular that a wave of wine counterfeiters arose in various parts of Europe. The first laws regulating local wine production, storage and shipping here were passed during the late Middle Ages.

As further incentive to local production in this area, as early as the fifteenth century, the wine trade was deemed so important to the local economy that wines for export were not taxed in the country where they were produced.

Foreigners – especially the English – received special dispensation too, financially. Records show that in addition to the British, there were merchants here from other areas, including Portugal and Genoa. Over 150 foreign traders were listed as doing business in this region during the sixteenth and seventeenth centuries. Some brokered wines for their home countries, while others were simply merchants and traders seeking a profitable business. Britain was a major consumer of wines from Jerez because the British Isles were not suitable for wine-grape growing at that time. Brittany had a similar problem, and welcomed the wines of the southern Iberian Peninsula. Flanders was also a very strong market, being another country that had a climate too cold to support the growth of wine grapes.

In the fifteenth century the fortification process for wine had become well known, after originating in Catalonia, a region that is now split between northern Spain and southern France. Geoffrey Chaucer, writing at the end of the 1300s, knew the wines of southern Spain. Wines from various countries were beginning to be fortified to increase their stability during the long weeks required to sail from their sources in southern Europe to customers in northern Europe and the British Isles. At that time sherries were fortified just before they were loaded into barrels for export.

In England, sherry wine was commonly served in taverns well before the mid-1500s. William Shakespeare knew this wine as 'sherris sack' or just plain 'sack', and he mentions it 35 times in his plays. Much speculation has been printed as fact to explain the term 'sack'. Some authors claim that sack is related to *sec*, the French word for 'dry' – referring to dry sherry wine. However, at that time, French was not even a common language in the whole area of what is now known as France, let alone a language used in the southern Iberian Peninsula. Others have stated that 'sack' is derived from the Spanish *sacar*, meaning to take, or to draw out, because this is the Spanish verb used when wine is withdrawn from barrels to be bottled before shipping. However, in the fifteenth and sixteenth centuries glassware was not common, and even if there were wine bottles, they would have been too costly and too fragile to use for shipping. But it does seem likely that the name did derive from the Spanish word *sacar*, referring to the extraction and transfer of wine from its ageing barrels to shipping barrels – no glass bottles involved at that time – which is a strong argument in favour of this theory.

No matter what it was called in England, sherry wine was increasingly sought after in many countries, from Italy to Ireland, by the mid-sixteenth century. Soon after their occupation, Portugal's African colonies also began importing sherry wines. Not too long after that, a market for sherry developed on the American continent. Many of the very early explorers and adventurous settlers had come from Portugal and Spain, where sherry was, of course, well known.

With the widening popularity of this wine, the name 'sherry' (as opposed to 'sack') became more standardized throughout the world. Sherry continued to be exported at a great rate through the seventeenth and eighteenth centuries, keeping up with worldwide demand despite political conflicts and economic uncertainties in Spain. Though British sherry imports decreased in the seventeenth century owing to various political conflicts, other countries seem to have made up the difference.

Throughout Europe, wine production methods had begun to improve in the late 1600s owing to increases in population, prosperity and demand. Wine quality improvements in Bordeaux created competition for sherry, as did the port industry in Portugal. And it wasn't just the types of wine, but the amounts of available wines which increased at that point. In addition to France, wine was now being produced everywhere from the Canary Islands to Madeira, from Italy to Greece.

By the eighteenth century quality demands from traders and consumers could no longer be ignored in Jerez. Necessary technological and commercial improvements began to be implemented in all aspects of the sherry industry, from viticulture to vinification to commercial processes. Vineyards were defined, styles of sherry wines were codified, and markets analysed for potential and promotion.

Many people today assume that the English always drank sweet sherry, because that's what they have seen at elderly relatives' homes, or on supermarket shelves. However, the first exported wines were dry, the same style enjoyed by the inhabitants of the area. The English shifted towards richer and sweeter sherries once high-quality dry wines had become readily available from France or other ports that were nearer to the British Isles.

British export merchants continued to enjoy a privileged trading status in the Jerez area, introduced by statute in 1645 and reinforced by additional treaties between Spain and Britain in 1667, 1713 and 1731. Wine exporters were also favoured by systems of payment for grapes which gave all the power and profit to the merchants, and little or nothing to the Spanish grape growers who supplied them – despite the fact that some of the Spanish suppliers were landowners, not tenants. Spanish vineyard owners were frustrated by not being able to break into the mercantile export system in any significant way. They were suffering under the British protectionist treaties, and felt unable to fully capitalize on the sherry trade themselves. So they set up vintners' guilds (*Gremios*) in the three major sherry-producing towns: in Jerez in 1733, in Sanlúcar de Barrameda in 1735 and in El Puerto de Santa María in 1745. Yet in the long run, the Gremios may have done as much harm as good.

It had not escaped the notice of Spanish wine producers that in certain circumstances, well-aged wines were becoming more valuable than new wines. This was the result, at least in part, of a worldwide demand for finer wines. There is documented evidence of the desirability of aged sherry as early as 1597, though aged wine of any type was extremely rare at that time.

Over a hundred years later, when the Gremios were founded, ageing wine was a little more common. But the Gremios did not want

A typical large, airy bodega, with workers placing barrels into rows for ageing sherry in the classic solera system.

the shippers to be the only people who made significant income from the sherry trade – leaving very little for the grape growers and wine producers. So the Gremios attempted to ensure that all the wine that was made in a given year was shipped out by a certain time, and at a certain minimum price. No one would be allowed to age sherry in Spain in order to sell it for a higher price. Thus wine merchants would not be able to profit from the sherry trade while leaving the growers and wine-producers with much less revenue after all their hard labour.

The new Gremio laws made it illegal for anyone other than Spanish, grape-growing landowners to store and age wines. It was a reasonable protection to demand. However, because of the existing balance of power, the Gremio laws proved impossible to enforce, even among Spanish wine dealers, let alone foreign merchants. So once again, the Spanish vineyard owners were left to fend for themselves – and their tenant farmers were even worse off.

Later in the eighteenth century, the Gremios' very existences were severely threatened, partly by the wine merchants flouting their regulations, and partly by a court case brought by one of the major sherry producers of the time, the Frenchman Juan Haurie. (Haurie's business eventually came to be called Domecq, which is still an eminent name in the sherry industry.) The result of the court case was quite significant, especially in its interpretation. The Gremios were not dissolved, but a new royal decree in January 1778 allowed sherry merchants to import some wines from outside the Marco de Jerez (Sherry Triangle) in order to 'colour' the wines to meet the demands of different international markets. This decree implicitly allowed the storage of wines because it is only during the wines' ageing in storage that the 'colour' wines were added.

Another result of this shake-up was room for more new and improved processes in every part of the sherry industry. The large number of styles of sherry being customized for different countries made it necessary to update everything from the methods under which the wines were produced and aged to the accounting and export regulations of the sherry merchants. In Andalusia the residents continued to enjoy their light, dry fino-style sherries, while most of the richer and sweeter styles were exported.

Because the wines were now aged in Spain before export, during the last few decades of the eighteenth century, large, airy bodegas (wine warehouses) began to arise in Jerez, as well as in Sanlúcar de Barrameda and El Puerto de Santa Maria. Some bodegas were located in the centre of the town of Jerez. Some sat near the seaport or river port in the other towns, because they were more convenient for export – though the commercial heart of the sherry business was in Jerez.

Bodegas are critical to the ageing process for sherry. Barrels of sherries are lined up in neat rows on the floors, and several tiers of barrels are balanced on top of them. The ceilings are very high – many metres above the highest tier of barrels – so there is ample room for fresh air to circulate through the bodegas, which is an essential aspect of the development of sherry wine. In each wall windows are opened or closed according to temperature and humidity conditions. From long practice, the winemakers know how much additional humidity – or drying winds – the developing sherries require during every period of the year.

These sizeable bodegas soon became emblematic of the whole sherry industry. In fact, sherry companies themselves tend to be referred to as 'bodegas', much as French wine producers are called 'chateaux' in Bordeaux. Many sherry bodegas are still in existence today in the Sherry Triangle towns, unmistakable with their high, white stucco walls, curlicued rooflines and colourful trim, the buildings and courtyards often embellished by lovely flower gardens and cascading stands of effusive, purple-pink bougainvillea.

This transition to ageing sherries in bodegas in Spain inadvertently helped the sherry trade during what could have been one of its darkest periods: the appearance of the dreaded grapevine plague phylloxera, which emerged here at the very end of the nineteenth century, in 1894. As it did everywhere in Europe, phylloxera devastated the vineyards. Because there is no cure, all the vineyards had to be replanted with special American rootstock, with the appropriate Spanish wine grape cuttings grafted on top.

Replanting, and waiting until the grapevines were old enough to produce, took a number of years. As phylloxera had appeared in Jerez quite late, the remedy was already known when it occurred, and the recovery time was shorter here than in some other wine regions. Of course, there was still a significant cost in money and time, which dealt another extreme blow to small vineyard owners and tenant farmers. But the larger bodega-owners – who were usually not vineyard owners – had enough stock of maturing barrels of sherry wines to continue to blend and release their aged wines during the time it took for the vineyards to recover and begin producing again.

The sherry trade was beginning to solidify in a modern way, with three tiers of suppliers. First were the grape-growers, those who owned or leased vineyards. The growers often made the basic wine too – pressing the grapes right in the fields as they were harvested. At the top level were the shippers, who blended, stored and aged differing amounts of wine before export depending on their level of expertise, their investment capital and the size of their bodegas. But not all shippers had the resources necessary for blending and ageing all the wines they would ship. So there was a third, interme-diate tier called the *almacenistas*. The *almacenistas* had large storage areas where they collected the wines from the grower-winemakers, and held them in ageing rooms where they were able to age and sometimes even custom-blend wines for the shipping companies. Over time, the *almacenistas* grew to be greatly respected, much like the *négociants* in France: they were connected to everyone in the business, and they had deep knowledge of the quality and quantity of all the wines, both before and after fortification and ageing.

In other areas of the globe, sherry imitators continued to spring up – as is always the case with successful wines. Some imitation came about by reason of geography: winemakers in South Africa and Australia began to produce their own 'sherries' because they

Sherry barrels being taken by horse-drawn conveyance to river docks teeming with small boats, ready to carry the wine out to larger seagoing cargo ships.

Postcard showing sherry wine being transported by oxcart to the Valdespino bodega, to be made into sherry.

A.R. VALDESPINO y Hⁿᵒ
Jerez de la Frontera.

Nº13. Carreta conduciendo mosto.   Charrette transportant du moût.

were so far from Spain that import costs were prohibitive for such a fashionable yet familiar drink. Other merchants simply wanted to make money from this extremely popular beverage, and they produced their own sherry-style wines from any number of fruits or vegetables, laced with components that mimicked the fortification and ageing of sherry – at least to untutored palates. With the trend towards sweeter sherry, this style was even simpler to copy: one only needed sugar, alcohol and whatever other flavourings and colours worked to fool the populace.

It was not difficult to sell this counterfeit sherry. One reason was its lower price. Another was that a significant percentage of sherry consumers were under the impression that 'sherry' was simply a category of drink, not a wine produced under explicit regulations in one particular, denominated area of Spain. Especially in Britain and British-based cultures, sherry became so ubiquitous by the end of the nineteenth century and through the middle of the twentieth that if pubs began to serve a large swathe of their most frugal customers inexpensive imitation 'sherries', who was to know, or care?

This was the impetus for the creation of a new regulating body for sherry in Spain. Sherry producers determined to define the borders of the Marco de Jerez (Sherry Triangle), as well as protocols to cover every aspect of sherry wine making from growing to production, labelling and export, including vineyards, grapes, vinification, ageing and styles of sherries. But it would take many decades for this to be accomplished.

Though Jerez was a centre for sherry merchants, it was not an obvious trade capital because it is situated about 20 kilometres (12 mi.) from the Atlantic coast. However, Jerez had already been an important commercial centre for centuries before it was defined by sherry – or before sherry defined the city; it could be said that either one was true by this time.

Historically, shippers had maintained their ready-for-export sherries in port cities, either near the Atlantic Ocean or at the mouth of a river leading to the ocean. The two major towns that served this function for sherry merchants were El Puerto de Santa María and Sanlúcar de Barrameda. Sherry was exported either by ships that sailed down the Guadalquivir River from Seville, picking up wines that were stored near the shoreline in Sanlúcar de Barrameda, or by ships that came in from the Atlantic, up the mouth of the Guadalete River, to docks at El Puerto de Santa María.

This began to change in the nineteenth century, when increasing stores of sherry were accumulating in the bodegas of Jerez and had to be conveyed to the ports by oxcarts or mules. Finally, in 1854, a railway was built from Jerez to El Puerto de Santa María. But the docks there were old, and there was no shelter nearby, so in 1870 a railway was built from Jerez to Cádiz, where larger, more modern ships could take on the wine barrels.

El Puerto de Santa María remained an integral part of the sherry production zone. But Sanlúcar de Barrameda became even more significant after the distinction was made among the sherries that were aged in the three different towns. It was discovered that wines aged by the ocean in Sanlúcar's distinctive micro-climate, with its temperate humidity, evolved into an exquisitely delicate version of fino sherry. This wine became so prized that it was given its own name and its own denomination: manzanilla. Though there are competing explanations for the name, the most likely explanation is that at some point the wine was distinguished as being as fine and fragrant as *manzanilla* (chamomile) flowers.

Also during this period, wine was beginning to be sold and shipped in bottles, not only in barrels. However, it would take another hundred years – until the 1980s – for this custom to fully take over and become required by regulation. One of the most famous sherry companies in the world made its name with custom-bottled wines in England: Harvey's of Bristol, producer of the legendary Harvey's Bristol Cream. This company, like many others at the time, imported and bottled its own branded blends of sherry. Harvey's became so ubiquitous that its most prominent wine (before Bristol Cream) was called 'Bristol Milk', equating it to a necessity of life.

Even with all this publicity, the problem of counterfeit 'sherries' was still rampant. So the sherry producers continued to work on creating a new body to regulate the area of production, as well as the vineyards and grapes, the winemaking and ageing – everything necessary to produce a true sherry in the Jerez area. They began in earnest in the early twentieth century, proposing their first denomination of origin designation in 1914.

However, at that time, the country of Spain did not have an effective body to oversee wineries and winemaking; that entity was not created until 1932, and it did not become a legal, governmental body until May 1933. Once that had been effected, national wine 'denominations of origin' could be put into place. In 1934 sherry became the first wine in Spain to have a legally authorized Denominación de Origen (Denomination of Origin) or DO. The DO was officially named Jerez-Xérès-Sherry, reflecting the history of both the sherry trade and the region itself, with its Spanish, Moorish and British influences. But over the next few years, various stakeholders succeeded in changing some aspects of the regulated area – and changing it back, too – several times. The first DO rules were eventually finalized in April 1936.

Probably the most famous sherry (outside of Spain), Harvey's Bristol Cream is still a favourite in many countries today. Its popularity is set to rise again as sherry is being used in more cocktails.

Vineyards

Most bodega owners historically did not own vineyards. They began as shippers, and were supplied either directly by growers or indirectly by *almacenistas*. Now there are about 3,000 growers in the Marco de Jerez and most of them belong to the seven major wine cooperatives in the area.

Currently there are 10,500 hectares (about 26,000 acres) of vineyards in the Marco de Jerez, mainly situated on gentle slopes.

Vineyards in the Sherry Triangle in the 1800s, with the winery strategically located nearby in order to press the grapes right after harvest in the hot sun.

To grow the Palomino grapes which are used for the dry sherries, the best vineyards are on hills of albariza soil (white clay and chalk) that is typical in certain parts of the region. Because of the decrease in the acreage of sherry vineyards and the continuing upgrades in sherry regulations during the twentieth century, at this time about 80 per cent of the vineyards carry the highest designation.

Climate-wise, the summer is a very dry period in terms of rainfall, though there is often humidity in the air from the nearby Atlantic Ocean. In addition, the white colour of the earth helps reflect back summer's hot sun, keeping the vineyards marginally cooler. Provisions for keeping the soil moist are made each autumn, when small berms of soil are built up in rectangles in the vineyards, in order to hold the winter rainfall until it can soak into the earth. After the winter, the soil in the vineyards is raked out level again. This time-consuming process, unique to the Jerez region, is called *aserpa* or *alumbra*.

Grapes

Until the phylloxera grapevine plague destroyed the vineyards of the Marco de Jerez in the late nineteenth century, there were dozens of different grapes grown in the area. Since replanting, there have basically been only three grapes used in the production of sherry: Palomino, Moscatel and Pedro Ximénez.

Palomino (also known as Palomino Fino) is a grape known elsewhere in the world as Listán. It is used for over 90 per cent of sherry production today: dry sherry in a variety of styles. The name of the grape supposedly came from a military man who served under King Alfonso x during the Reconquista; the soldier, Fernan Ibañez Palomino, is believed to have settled in Jerez in the thirteenth century.

Another local grape, Pedro Ximénez, is mainly used for making sweet wines. It was purportedly brought to Jerez by Peter Siemens, a Dutch soldier employed by King Carlos v in the early sixteenth century. Pedro Ximénez is thought to be the name of this Dutchman translated into the local language: a nice legend, if unprovable so far. The name of the grape is often abbreviated to px.

There is also a very small amount of a grape known here as Moscatel, a grape that is known elsewhere as Muscat of Alexandria. Moscatel grapes can be used only in wines that are labelled as Moscatel; these are all sweet sherries.

The Consejo Regulador do Jerez-Xérès-Sherry, which was established in the 1930s, is the trade consortium that oversees every step of the sherry wine process, from vineyards through vinification to storage and ageing. During the harvest period, for example, the Consejo monitors grape yields, the quality of the grapes harvested and even the pressure applied in the grape presses.

Solera System

All sherries are aged in the solera system. The word 'solera' refers to the floor of the bodega where the barrels of wine are placed on their sides to age. The technical term for this type of ageing is 'fractional blending'.

After fermentation, the fortified wine is placed in barrels, about four-fifths full. The barrels are placed in rows on the floors (soleras) of the large, unheated and uncooled, high-ceilinged bodegas (which are above-ground 'wine cellars' or wine-ageing warehouses). At that point, the indigenous *flor* (flower), a fluffy, white film of special yeast, grows naturally on the surface of the wines destined to be dry sherries. Though it is a type of yeast, the flor does not restart the conversion of sugars to alcohol. Instead, the flor acts as an insulator, remaining in place while the wine develops further, interacting slightly with the wine, but mainly forming a barrier between the wine and the air, so that the sherry develops 'biologically' and without significant oxidation.

Sherry for bottling is always removed from the bottom level of barrels, which are then refilled from the next level above. Then the second-level barrels are refilled from the level above, and so on. Wine barrels on the top layer receive the new wines each year. Commonly, the stacks are three or four barrels high, but they can go up to six, or sometimes even ten or twelve levels high.

The barrels above the solera layer are the *criadera* or ageing layers. This can be confusing because sometimes the word 'criadera' also refers to the ageing process. Sometimes the entire ageing process is called *solera-criadera*. No matter the name, it is all the same process.

Another important phenomenon that occurs during sherry ageing is evaporation. Typically, sherries evaporate at a rate of up to 6 per cent every year, averaging 4.5 per cent annually. This has the effect of concentrating the flavours and aromas of the wines, and of slowly increasing the percentage of alcohol in the wines. Though most sherries are sold at 15–18 per cent alcohol, long-aged sherries can reach 20 per cent ABV (alcohol by volume) or higher. In recent years, some of the wealthier bodegas have taken steps to make their ageing rooms more airtight in order to decrease the amount of evaporation. This is an expensive procedure, and it flies in the face of tradition. So far, the effect on sherry ageing has not been fully measured, and wisdom of this process has not yet been determined.

Sherry Styles and their Vinification

Within the solera system there are two tracks: biological and oxidative ageing. The first literally employs biological yeast as a barrier between the wine and oxygen. The second track allows a controlled amount of oxygenation in the ageing process.

But before all this, the vinification process must take place. Because most sherry today is dry, and is made with the Palomino grape, that will be discussed first.

Fino and Manzanilla

Palomino grapes have very thin skins that split easily, so historically, the presses went to the grapes instead of the other way around: Palomino grapes were often pressed right in the vineyards. If not in the vineyards, the presses had to be very close by because the instant the grapes split open, the juice begins to oxidize – especially in the sun-drenched September heat in the Marco de Jerez. Though the end-product of sherry is an oxidized wine, the oxidation process only occurs after the grapes have been fermented into wine and the wine has been fortified, ready for ageing.

The 'lightest' style of sherry, fino (fine), is made with mainly free-run juice, which means that after these thin-skinned grapes have been destemmed, they sit in the press as their weight crushes any remaining whole grapes to release the juice; a very light pressing may complete the process. Nowadays, the juice is collected into tanks and immediately cooled to prevent premature oxidation while waiting for the rest of the harvest to come in to fill the tanks. Only then will fermentation begin.

After the 'first-press' juice is collected, there is a second pressing. All the grape juice (also known as must) is kept separately, according to whether it is the first, second or remainder pressing. Each pressing

Super-modern labelling on a fino sherry from the traditional firm of Sánchez Romate.

Manzanilla, a special, delicate form of fino sherry, can only be made in the town of Sanlúcar in the Sherry Triangle. Here, it is sold in several sizes for convenience.

is destined for a different style of wine. The first pressing, which is about 65 per cent of the total, is used for fino and manzanilla wines – those that are biologically aged. The second pressing is used for wines that are aged oxidatively. The rest of the must may be used to make *rayas* wines that can be used to 'strengthen' certain styles of sherry. Or the unfortified juice may be boiled down to one-fifth of its original volume and used to add colour to certain sherries; this product is called *arrope*.

Today, most sherry wines are fermented in stainless steel using modern winemaking techniques such as temperature control, filtration, pH correction and clarification at various stages of the vinification process. A small amount of sherry is still fermented in fairly new wooden barrels for a short while, for the purpose of 'seasoning' the barrels. This process is actually 'de-seasoning', using the wine to absorb the major aromas and flavours from the wood, because it is necessary to have 'neutral' barrels in order to properly age sherry wines.

Sherry barrels are traditionally made of American oak, which is larger-grained than French oak. This custom apparently began shortly after the discovery of America, when many raw goods were sourced in North America for European manufacturers and consumers. In the sherry trade barrels are known as 'butts'. After some historical variations, butts have been standardized to hold about 500 litres (around 132 gallons). Historically, sherry wine was fermented in oak barrels, as well as being aged in them.

The fermentation begins using either natural, indigenous yeasts that are present on the grapes, or by inoculating the must with either specially selected natural yeasts or purchased yeasts; the choice is made by the winemaker. After fermentation, the finished, unfortified wines are required to have a minimum alcohol level of 10.5 per cent.

Once the wines have been fermented and clarified, the winemaker makes another choice, based on organoleptical factors apparent to an experienced sherry-maker; he or she decides which wines will become fino or manzanilla wines, and which are destined to be oloroso wines. Fino and manzanilla wines (called *sobretabla* at this stage) will undergo biological ageing, while olorosos will undergo oxidative ageing. Before ageing, the wines destined to be fino or manzanilla sherries are fortified with natural grape alcohol to a level of 15.5 per cent alcohol, which kills the fermenting yeasts and brings the alcoholic fermentation to an end.

The wines are put into barrels that are about four-fifths full, and the barrels are laid on their sides in large, airy bodegas. The bodegas must be located within specified areas of the Marco de Jerez, where all sherries must be aged. Manzanillas can only be aged in Sanlúcar de Barrameda, while finos can also be produced and aged in Jerez and El Puerto de Santa María.

Fino and manzanilla wines are both aged under a veil of flor, the layer of yeast that completely covers the surface of the wine, interacting with the wine below it and the oxygen above it, in order to extract the nutrients that sustain it. Over the years, the flor contributes more complexity to the sherries. In the humid, seaside air of Sanlúcar, manzanillas develop under a thick layer of flor year-round, while in other parts of the Sherry Triangle, the flor thins out in the cool winters and the hot summers.

A bit more fresh fino wine is added to the barrels periodically, usually twice a year, to provide nutrients for the flor. To produce manzanillas, the wines are very carefully monitored and very small amounts of fresh wine are added much more frequently, in order to preserve the thickness of the all-important layer of flor on the sherry. This takes place within the solera, or fractional ageing, system.

For fino and manzanilla wines, up to one-third of the wine may be taken from the bottom or 'solera' level of barrels in the bodega each year. The wines are filtered and fined again before bottling. Minimum fino ageing has been reduced from three years in barrel to two, officially, though many higher-end finos are aged longer. Most finos are a light straw-gold in colour, while some have green or gold tints; the longer-aged wine is deeper in colour.

Finos are light and piquant, stimulating to the appetite as is fitting, because they are considered aperitif wines, often sipped with tapas. Manzanilla wines are also aperitif wines. They are light straw-coloured, and considered more ethereal, being slightly salty and delicately tangy.

Once the finos and manzanillas are aged for several years they are bottled; at that point they are ready to be sold and consumed. Some fino sherries and certain manzanillas may be aged as much as twice as long; they are released on the market when the winemaker judges them to be ready.

This is a new style of the delicate manzanilla sherry: en rama. It is unfiltered and slightly earthier than traditional manzanilla. En rama sherry is also vintage-specific, usually released in late spring or early summer, and made to be consumed during the year when it is released.

En Rama and Seasonal Sherries

Lately it has become popular to bottle some sherries without their final filtration, which yields a sherry referred to as *en rama* (raw). This treatment allows the sherry to continue to interact with the tiny, even microscopic particles that continue to enrich the wine's flavours. En rama sherries can be said to follow the current trend towards more natural practices in wine. They are often bottled in the spring, perhaps because it is traditional to wait until after the winter, when the flor thins and even disappears, to bottle finos and manzanillas. The en rama wines do have a different aromatic and flavour profile from the fully filtered and fined versions; they are somewhat rounder, stronger and earthier, which is sometimes very noticeable, and other times incrementally apparent. There is little colour difference between the two in young wines; more is visible in the older wines.

Only recently, some producers have begun to bottle very small amounts of sherries in different seasons. The producers are offering consumers the opportunity to taste what sherry is like at various times of the year, reflecting seasonal changes in the flor. The 'seasonal' sherries are fino- or manzanilla-style wines, fortified and aged but bottled and released as soon as is allowed by DO regulation: these wines are made to appeal to discerning white wine consumers, to be enjoyed as aperitifs.

There can some confusion between en rama and seasonal sherries. Sherries cannot be vintage dated because they are made with the solera system, which blends together many vintages during ageing. A clear date on a label is one indicator of an en rama or seasonal sherry. However, that is the bottling date, not the vintage (harvest) date that other (non-sherry) wines display on their labels. Seasonal sherries may have a season printed on their labels. Both bottling dates and seasonal names are there to encourage consumption as soon as possible. The wines are young and bright, best served chilled, and consumed within a couple of days of opening the bottle.

Though the first en rama sherries that came on the market in recent years were finos or manzanillas celebrated for their freshness, in fact any producer can bottle any sherry en rama, which is something like the designation of 'cask strength' in the whisky world. For sherry, it does not necessarily indicate that the wine has a different percentage of alcohol, but simply means that the sherry is as close to 'cask taste' as it can be while still being stable in the bottle.

Pasada

At the opposite end of the spectrum are wines labelled 'Pasada' which indicates wines that have more age than is usual for this type of wine. For example, 'Manzanilla Pasada' means that this wine has aged past the time when it would have normally been bottled; in this case, past the time when its flor has finally dissipated. Confusingly, Manzanilla Pasada can also be bottled en rama. In this case, en rama refers to the wine being bottled with less filtration than normal.

Amontillado

Every barrel of sherry is different, and there is often no clear explanation for why one develops differently from the barrel next to it. Sometimes the flor on a fino or manzanilla begins to thin out earlier than expected. Once the wine is no longer insulated from air by the flor, the wine can be affected by oxygen. In other words, the wine begins to undergo oxidative ageing. A sherry that has been aged partially biologically (under flor) and partially oxidatively becomes an amontillado. The term *amontillado* dates from the latter eighteenth century, and it is thought to derive from Montilla, a nearby wine region where the flor did not last as long during the ageing process.

Strictly speaking, *amontillado* sherries are dry. Their flavours are clean, but the wine is a bit more intense, toastier and nuttier than fino or manzanilla. In the past, some amontillado wines were sweetened but today consumers prefer the wines to be dry. Amontillados are also darker tan in colour than finos or manzanillas.

It is theoretically possible to create an amontillado by adding a bit more alcohol to a fino or manzanilla, which kills the special yeast that creates the layer of flor. Or a producer could refrain from refreshing the fino or manzanilla barrels with new wine during the year, which would cause the flor layer to thin out and die. And if it's possible to do this, of course it has been done. But not, of course, in the current Marco de Jerez under the DO regulations.

An oloroso sherry that happens to be produced in El Puerto de Santa María, the least well known of the three towns in the Sherry Triangle.

Oloroso

Oloroso sherries are also aged in the solera-criadera system, but in an oxidative manner, without the layer of flor on the wine. Before they are aged, olorosos are fortified to 17–18 per cent alcohol so the fermentation ends, and not even a layer of flor can grow on the wine. The wines are put in barrels, and the surfaces of the wines are exposed to some air (oxygen). The interaction with the barrels also affects the colours, aromas and flavours of the wines, enriching them over the years. In fact, the word 'oloroso' refers to the wine being aromatic.

Finished olorosos are slightly higher in alcohol because they are aged longer, and some evaporation of the liquid takes place, concentrating the flavours. This aspect of the process also darkens them to rich shades of a golden, light or medium brown, depending on their age. They are mouth-fillingly rich, so rich that they may seem to have a touch of sweetness, but ultimately the wines are dry.

Palo Cortado

Palo cortado sherry has an almost mythic quality. Historically, it was a rare artefact of the sherry-making process, a higher-alcohol, richer, delicately dry wine. During the fermentation process for fino sherries, after tasting the wine, a winemaker would occasionally find a barrel of fino he determined to be so extraordinary it was anointed as future palo cortado. The barrel would be handled separately from the fino wines, with corrective fortification added as necessary during its ageing.

Today, finos are fermented in large tanks, so producing a palo cortado is now done by intent, not by chance. A winemaker can

select out a small amount of fino – perhaps from a special year or a special vineyard area – and treat it separately, fortifying it and beginning its ageing under flor but quickly adding small amounts of additional fortification as necessary. It's a difficult process to keep the wine light and balanced during its ageing.

Historically, it may be that before the phylloxera epidemic limited the number of grape varieties in sherry (and before large-tank fermentation) it was easier to find more diversity in the vineyards and their resultant wines. No matter: palo cortado is still considered to be a rare and wonderful sherry, even with modern winemaking methods. The finished wine displays grace and subtlety, yet has a pronounced body and structure.

Rather than the fairy-tale meaning one might expect for this sherry's name, the words *palo cortado* simply mean 'cut stick', referring to the mark a winemaker would put on his chosen barrels. There is an elaborate marking system for sherry barrels in general: sticks and cross-hatches, check-marks that are called hen's feet, and other traditional symbols, each with its own time-honoured name in the local jargon.

Pedro Ximénez

Pedro Ximénez sweet sherries are, of course, made with Pedro Ximénez grapes. The grapes are harvested later in the season, in order to ripen – or even overripen – them to their maximum sugar content. Immediately after harvest, the grapes are laid out on straw mats right in the vineyards. This process is called *soleo*, and its purpose is for *pasificación* (from *pasa* which means raisin) to evaporate moisture, concentrating the grapes' aromas and flavours, and allowing the wine to have more sweetness, more fruitiness and more density on the palate.

The grape bunches are turned over by hand every day for at least a week, and sometimes more than two weeks. During that time, any sub-par grapes are revealed and removed. Then the grapes are pressed and the wine begins its slow alcoholic fermentation,

Lighting shows off the medium amber hues of the relatively rare palo cortado, a sherry that is rich yet light.

which lasts for some weeks during the autumn and into the winter. When this process is finished, the wines are fortified to 15–17 per cent alcohol, racked off their lees and aged in a solera system. A finished Pedro Ximénez sherry is an incredibly rich wine, redolent of raisins and figs, concentrated and abundant on the palate.

Because most vineyards in the Marco de Jerez have now been determined to be far more suitable to grow Palomino grapes, a substantial amount of Pedro Ximénez grapes are now grown in nearby Montilla-Moriles, an adjacent region where PX flourishes. This region currently carries special dispensation to supply fresh Pedro Ximénez wine to be used in refreshing the Pedro Ximénez soleras in the Sherry Triangle.

Moscatel

While sweet Moscatel sherries were very popular in the past, and were considered excellent, today there are very few fine Moscatel sherries made. Moscatel grapes are mainly grown in the sandy soil around Chipiona, a small town within the Marco de Jerez. When the Moscatel grapes are dried like the Pedro Ximénez grapes, the wines are called *moscateles pasas*. These days, very old Moscatels are rare and can be amazingly wonderful. Notably, Valdespino's Toreles is considered miraculous at nearly a hundred years old, but only tiny amounts of this sherry are occasionally bottled and released these days.

Añada

Very occasionally, if a producer acquires wine from an exceptional vintage, the bodega will keep a small amount of it aside for separate ageing after vinification and fortification. This means years of caring for a special selection, and optimizing its ageing without sherry's traditional solera system. After ageing, if the sherry meets all relevant criteria it can be bottled and labelled with a vintage date, and be classified as DO Añada sherry.

Wine Categories

There are three wine categories that sherries are divided into, overall. *Vinos generosos* include fino, manzanilla, amontillado, palo cortado and oloroso. *Vinos dulces naturales* are Pedro Ximénez and Moscatel. *Vinos generosos de licor* are a blend of the first two categories and most proprietary blends of sherries fall into this category, with names such as East India, Bristol Milk, Pale Cream and Bristol Cream. Some of these terms are rare or antiquated, while others are still popular today.

Tradition, Cocktails and Value

Among aged wines, lately, sherry has been one of the best value. The prices are just starting to creep up as quality and international awareness increase. Still, in a restaurant, an aperitif sherry or a dessert sherry by the glass is generally quite reasonably priced. This also occurs because wine directors who have newly encountered these wines are eager to share their sherry discoveries with customers.

Traditionally, sherry was taken in small glasses, sipped before a meal, either luncheon or dinner, especially in British and British-influenced cultures. The early sherries were fairly dry, but sweeter ones crept in as the centuries progressed. By the first part of the 1800s, most sherries imported to Britain were sweet. These sweet sherries were then considered 'women's drinks'. By this time, the men had replaced their sweet dessert sherries with port (and sometimes other European sweet wines). Women traditionally did not drink port.

By the time sherry's popularity plummeted in the latter half of the twentieth century, hundreds of years of British sherry tradition were in thorough disarray. Though some people favoured the richer sherries as a lunch aperitif, many people (especially women) even drank sweet (not dry) sherry in the morning. Except in Spain, most people had forgotten how wonderfully piquant and appetite-inspiring dry sherries can be.

But around the turn of the twenty-first century the sherry market did begin to recover, though in a different iteration. Today, there are more fine, dry sherries on fine wine shop shelves, so it's much easier to avoid the inexpensive bottles of dubious quality. And though it's true that a bottle of sherry will last for weeks once it's opened, it will not last indefinitely and should be refrigerated to preserve quality.

In Spain, and in some other areas of the world, both dry and sweet sherries are being offered in smaller-sized bottles such as 50 cl (500 ml) or half-bottles (375 ml). Buying these sizes is a wonderful technique to use when sampling the newer, better sherries. Since sherry is fairly hardy, it's not too difficult to find bottles of wine that have remained in good condition. The best, of course, will be from reputable wine shops. Most sherry is not vintage-dated, but the newly popular en rama sherries have a bottling date on their labels to enable consumers to drink them at their peak. They are not as stable as other sherries so it is best to purchase and consume these within a year.

Sherry is made to be consumed when it is released for sale. Further ageing is not required. It's best to drink sherry within a year or two of purchase. An unopened bottle can be stored standing up in a dark, cool place. Sweet sherry will last longer in the bottle, either unopened or opened. But after opening, storing the bottles in the refrigerator and finishing them within a few weeks ensures optimum quality.

Traditionally, sherries were served in small glasses. Centuries ago, wine glasses were many times smaller than those of today, but sherry traditions have kept servings small and sippable. Most often, sherries were served close to 16°C (60°F) – considered 'room

The venerable firm of Harvey's of Bristol, famous for 'Bristol Cream' and 'Bristol Milk', also produces drier and finer sherries such as this aged palo cortado.

temperature' before central heating proliferated. Some chilling is best for all sherries today. Along with the newer styles of en rama and seasonal sherries, fino and manzanilla sherries can be served a little colder, even over ice.

Sherry is traditionally consumed with tapas in Spain: small servings of sharpish cheese or smoked tuna are common in Jerez. Sometimes the plate is strewn with toasted Marcona almonds or pistachios, and drizzled with olive oil. This works well with fino and manzanilla, and delicate palo cortado sherries too. Moving to the richer sherries, amontillado and oloroso, these can pair nicely with heartier foods such as dry, cured sausages or potatoes with spicy sauces, and some roasted or stewed meats.

Almonds and pistachios come to the fore with sweet sherry pairings, as do other toasted nuts such as hazelnuts and walnuts, and also blue cheeses. Sweet sherries complement many cakes, as well as dessert dishes with flavours ranging from dried fig, apricot and raisin, through treacle and spun sugar, to chocolate.

Other Fortified Wines in Andalusia

Other regions within Andalusia have traditionally produced fortified wines but they have remained less significant than Jerez. Today there are two additional Andalusian denominated wine regions for fortified wines: DO Condado de Huelva to the west and DO Málaga to the east.

Málaga

Málaga is an important wine-producing area on the Mediterranean side of Andalusia. Its grapes are grown on the hillsides, inland from the sea. There are several tiers of fortified wines, aged slowly in American oak barrels. Because of the climate, the grapes tend to have a high sugar content. The finished wines are as high as 15 per cent alcohol without fortification, so some of the wines are never fortified.

But there are various styles of fortified DO Málaga wines: dry, semi-dry, semi-sweet and sweet. Several fortification processes are used to produce the sweeter wines. Those called *vino dulce natural* (natural sweet wine) are fortified near the beginning of the fermentation, resulting in a fresh and sweet style. *Vinos maestros* (master wines) are lightly fortified before fermentation, which results in a long and slow fermentation, and a finished sweet wine. *Vino tierno* (tender wine) is made with partially dried grapes; the grapes are pressed after drying in the sun for a week or two, then this must is fermented into wine, and fortified at a specified point so the wine retains some sweetness. (It should also be mentioned here that Málaga's Moscatel raisins are also PDO (Protected Designation of Origin) products in the EU; these are the same grapes used to make their Moscatel fortified wines.)

Finished fortified wines are age-designated. *Pálido* (pale) are aged up to six months. *Noble* wines are aged two to three years. *Añejos* are aged three to five years, and *trasañejo* wines are aged for over five years.

Colour is also important in designating Málaga's sweet wines. The wines darken during oxidative ageing, both from interaction with oxygen and from the wooden barrels in which they are stored. Winemakers are also allowed to add *arrope* (syrup made from concentrated wine grapes) for colour. Often this additive is used to conform to different consumer expectations in different markets.

The current authorized terms for Málaga's different styles of wines are influenced more by German, not English, because Germany has been a very important export market for Málaga's wines for more than fifty years. Spanish, German and English terms can currently be used on the wine labels as follows: wines labelled 'Dorado' or 'golden' are aged without *arrope* (grape syrup) being added for colour. 'Rojo dorado' or 'Rot gold' (red-gold) wines can have up to 5 per cent *arrope* added. 'Oscuro' or 'brown' (dark or brown) wines have between 5 and 10 per cent *arrope*. 'Colour' wines are commonly made with 10 to 15 per cent *arrope*. 'Negro' or 'Dunkel' (black or dark) wines, with over 15 per cent *arrope* added, are dark ebony, nearly black in colour. There are other subtle categories of Málaga wines with and without colour added, including *pajarete* (which may be dark in colour but has no *arrope* added); *lagrima* (made with free run, unpressed grape must); and *igualar*, which is also known as *assemblar* (blended).

Málaga wines may also be labelled with Spanish- or English-based names similar to those of sherries, including dry pale or pale dry, *naturalmente dulce* (naturally sweet), *dulce natural* (sweet natural), *dulce crema* or cream (sweet cream or cream), pale cream and sweet.

Huelva

Huelva was known for its fortified wines as early as the fifteenth century. One of its claims to fame is its 'Wines of Discovery', because Columbus took Huelva wines with him on his voyage to the New World in 1502. After that time, Huelva seems to have devolved into lesser importance on a national and international scale than Jerez. Some of the same Jerez grapes are grown in Huelva, and used to make fortified wines, but the important white grape here is Zalema. Additional white grapes that can also be used in DO Condado de Huelva wines are Palomino Fino, Listán de Condado de Huelva, Garrido Fino, Moscatel de Alejandria and Pedro Ximénez. Huelva wines have been produced under Spanish denomination of origin specifications since the DO was created in 1932 and legally established in 1933, with the first releases being labelled DO Huelva in 1934, at the same time as DO Jerez sherry.

Montilla-Moriles

There is one more significant region to mention in relation to sherry: Montilla-Moriles. This is a wine region in Andalusia that is located to the west of the Marco de Jerez. Some of the same grapes are grown here, but the wines are not fortified owing to their late ripening with high sugar content, and consequently high alcohol content in the wine. Especially notable are the unfortified sweet wines made with

the same Pedro Ximénez grape that is used in sherry. In fact some of the Pedro Ximénez wines are allowed to be imported into the Marco de Jerez to be used (fortified) in the solera process when there is not enough Pedro Ximénez wine available in the Marco de Jerez.

Málaga, another city in the Andalusia region of Spain where fortified wines are produced.

Cause and Effect in the International Sherry Trade

Persevering during the cycles of commerce during much of the twentieth century, the sherry trade expanded and contracted as export potential dictated. Within this time, however, several problems in this industry also persisted. One was the prevalence of non-Jerez-based sherry wines on the world market. As mentioned earlier, sherry-style producers abounded in other countries, especially those with ties to British culture. Some of the products were even given names like

'British sherry', 'South African sherry' or 'Australian sherry', which certainly sounded authentic in their own countries – as if it were Spanish sherry made in Jerez especially for a certain country. This was a reasonable assumption because at that time sherry was often still shipped in barrels from Spain, to be bottled on arrival in its new country.

As a result, many consumers were used to seeing an English name brand on their sherries. A 1967 court case in London brought this all out in public. There, it was finally acknowledged that 'real' sherry came from Spain. However, there had been sherry-style wines produced for so long that some of them were still allowed to be sold under their own brand names as well. A similar case was brought in the United States in the next decade, with a similar dual-track result.

It wasn't until after Spain became part of the European Union in 1986 that international protections for Denomination of Origin (DO) sherry were adopted. Even so, this name protection only applies to countries that are part of the EU. For all other countries, treaties must be negotiated separately. Forward-thinking Australians began to call their sherry-style wines 'apera' as of 2012. There, the producers have welcomed being able to market an entirely new wine product instead of struggling to move ahead with sherry's old-fashioned image. The name apera was created to suggest the fact that in Australia, sherries are usually served as aperitifs.

In the U.S., wine-related agreements are often left to be negotiated by each wine region – and there are hundreds. Some older U.S. 'sherry-style wine' producers have been exempted from these agreements on the grounds that they have been producing their own branded 'sherry' (or 'Champagne' or 'Burgundy', and so on) for so long that they are historic products with historic identities. It happens that these wines are often low in price and quality, with considerable profit to the producer, hence the producer's reluctance to let go of the name. At this time, it is unknown how long this phenomenon of historic artefact will continue.

In recent decades, the Consejo Regulador has done some updating and fine-tuning, tightening regulations and adding additional protocols where necessary. One is the definition of the denominated *crianza* (ageing) zone for sherry. DO sherry can be aged in Jerez de la Frontera, El Puerto de Santa María and Sanlúcar de Barrameda. However, as of 1964, DO manzanilla-Sanlúcar de Barrameda can only be aged in Sanlúcar. (And by practice, there is no fino aged in Sanlúcar.) The Consejo Regulador administers the production and ageing zones for grape growers, winemakers and those involved in the ageing, bottling and sales of sherries, including bodegas large and small, and the *almacenistas* (who may hold, blend and age sherries for the shippers).

It might seem surprising but the same Consejo Regulador that supervises the production of sherries also supervises the production of a type of vinegar. This is the unique Vinagre de Jerez, which has the same production zone as sherry as well as very specific regulations for production and ageing; its purview was added to the Consejo in 1994.

In the year 2000 one more very important element was added to the roster of sherry elements that is administered by this Consejo Regulador. That year marked the official recognition of two new categories of aged sherries: VOS and VORS. The official Latin names of these categories are *Vinum optimum signatum* and *Vinum optimum rare signatum*; unofficially they are referred to as 'very old sherry' and 'very old rare sherry'. VOS sherry must be at least twenty years old while VORS must be at least thirty. Some sherries had been aged for decades by the wines' producers, agers and/or shippers, but this was the first time the age of the sherry could be officially placed on the label. Buyers are currently placing a premium on aged sherries, as they are on aged wines of all types.

There is one hurdle that had to be overcome here: the definition of the age of the sherry was specified as the average age of the solera, but in the solera system, this is almost impossible to prove. However, the producers and the Consejo came up with a way to certify VOS and VORS. The wines must undergo three tests. One is laboratory testing, which includes carbon-14 dating. Another is the requirement that a bodega must have twenty or thirty times more sherry in stock than the amount they are bottling as VOS or VORS. And the third is an organoleptic assessment: each sherry must pass the test of five experienced tasters, one from the Consejo and four others who are oenologists or experts in the field, and not currently working at a bodega.

Bodegas

Most of today's producers blend and age as well as export their sherries. In addition, there are still many *almacenista* firms who remain anonymous to the public while storing, blending and/or ageing sherries for the major bodegas.

In recent decades there has been quite a bit of consolidation in sherry bodega ownership, and some new companies have also come to the fore in this industry. But many of the old names have been retained by their new owners. At this point in time, there are approximately eighty bodegas in the Sherry Triangle. Here is a sampling of the major names in sherry, both current and historic: Barbadillo, Bodegas Tradición, Delgado Zuleta, Álvaro Domecq, Pedro Domecq, Fernando de Castilla, César Florido, Fundador, Garvey, González Byass, Gutiérrez Colosía, Harveys, Emilio Hidalgo, Hidalgo-La Gitana, La Guita, Lustau, Osborne, Pedro Romero, Sánchez Romate, Sandeman, Urium, Valdespino, Valdivia and Williams & Humbert.

Postmodern Sherry

As mentioned earlier, en rama (literally 'raw') sherries, bottled with minimal filtering, have become fashionable. This may be a reflection of the natural wine movement, and/or of the trend towards more 'authentic' food. In any case, en rama wines are considered to be purer, less 'industrial' and more representative of true sherry flavours. However, it's important to know that en rama sherries are somewhat less stable than other sherries. They are not candidates for ageing, and should be consumed as soon as possible, within a matter of months after bottling – a year at the outside. In the recent en rama movement, fino was the first and most popular en rama sherry style, but the other styles have been jumping on the bandwagon now that en rama is becoming a coveted style.

Most of the new sherries are dry. Currently, fino and manzanilla are the most popular. Even amontillados and olorosos are being meticulously produced to feel rich in aromas and flavours, but finish dry on the palate. However, the sweet Pedro Ximénez wines are also valued by many winemakers and consumers. In fact one company has decided to specialize in this style of wine, renaming their company Ximénez-Spinola. The Spinola company first appeared on the Jerez landscape in 1729. This family concern was an *almacenista* before becoming a true bodega – bottling and labelling their own wines. The ninth generation now runs the company. Though they are one of the smallest bodegas in Jerez, they have some fascinating treasures in their older wines that they are starting to release now, to the delight of discerning wine-lovers.

While internationally, sherry (mainly dry) has become the darling of mixologists, there is still a strong tradition of 'house sherry' in many restaurants, cafes and bars throughout Jerez. It's common to stop in at the end of the day to relax with a small glass of dry sherry served with tapas such as local cheese, smoked tuna, ham or other small plates, often garnished with toasted, salted Marcona almonds. For those that aren't that hungry, the ubiquitous *picos* (crunchy, cylindrical crackers) are served in bowls and packets.

In Jerez, the lightest sherry can be ordered as 'vino fino de la casa' (fino house wine). Each establishment will have barrels placed in a corner of the room that they draw the sherries from. In addition to fino there will be amontillado and oloroso, and perhaps a small container of Pedro Ximénez for later, after the meal. Some of

'Nectar' is an elegantly modern dessert sherry made with Pedro Ximénez, by the venerable González Byass firm.

the sherries are made by well-known producers, while others are unlabelled when supplied to the restaurant; they are all especially enjoyable when paired with the house tapas.

During the warmer months, tables are set outside cafes so the adults can linger and chat while the children play nearby, in small plazas. Near the cafes on the main pedestrian street and in the main plaza in Jerez there is also a dynamic, brightly painted, hundred-year-old carousel, a lively two-storey amusement that attracts children, parents and grandparents throughout the evening.

Drinking Sherry Today

In the world of sherry, cocktails are only one part of its resurgence. Clever marketing has taken advantage of mixologists' strengthening interest to re-introduce sherry as a wine to be drunk on its own. Restaurant wine directors are enjoying selecting the right sherries to pair with different dishes at their establishments.

Another indication of the increasing popularity is the large number of entrants in the biennial Copa Jerez sherry and food-pairing competition. Organized by Fedejerez and the Consejo Regulador for DO Jerez-Xérès-Sherry, Copa Jerez invites teams of a chef-plus-sommelier from restaurants in seven countries – Germany, Belgium, Denmark, Spain, the United States, the Netherlands and the United Kingdom – to compete first in their own countries; then the national winners are flown to Jerez for the final, international competition.

The use of sherry in cocktails has been soaring worldwide. As evidenced by current mixology-oriented events such as New Orleans' annual Tales of the Cocktail, the legend of classic sherry cocktails is alive again, and inspiring bartenders to create additional sherry-based drinks every year. Sherry itself can contain most of the elements necessary for a complete cocktail: flavours that play off each other such as alcohol, fruit, bitterness, acidity and even sweetness. In certain countries, including the UK and U.S., there is also an annual sherry cocktail competition for bartenders.

Bartenders are now featuring cocktails with different styles of sherry. New versions add myriads of elements from bitters to tropical fruits. The most famous classic sherry cocktail of the past is the sherry cobbler, which can be made with any of the dry or rich (not sweet) sherry styles such as fino or amontillado, combined with simple syrup and orange or tropical fruit juice, shaken and served on the rocks.

For home mixologists there is a world of recipes online today. An easy way to start is with a simple cocktail of chilled, dry sherry: serve 90 ml (3 oz.) of chilled fino over ice; add a twist of lime or lemon. This works nicely with fino en rama as well.

4
Madeira

———— ◆ ————

Madeira is an almost mythical wine. Open a bottle that is a hundred years old and the wine will still be rich, aromatic and flavourful. Once uncorked, a bottle of Madeira can stay open for up to a year with the wine remaining fresh. Drinking Madeira is a cascade of experiences evoking tastes of salt, nuts, apples, citrus fruits and toffee.

Equally amazing is the scarcity of Madeira wine today, which contributes to its legendary reputation. Just as in the Middle Ages, when there were vague stories of unicorn sightings on the other side of the mountains, today it often seems that only friends of friends, or people in film and literature, have ever sipped Madeira wine. However, exports of Madeira are increasing again, so it's interesting to look at who is now consuming this rare wine. And what, in fact, is it?

Madeira is a fortified wine traditionally made with several types of white grapes that are considered indigenous to the island of Madeira – though wine grapes were brought to this former volcanic isle from the mainland in the early fifteenth century, after Madeira was 'discovered' by Portuguese explorers. This island is now part of Portugal, though it is situated well out in the Atlantic Ocean, 970 kilometres (600 mi.) southwest of Lisbon. It lies along a shipping route from Britain and Europe to Asia (before the Suez Canal was built) and from Europe to the West Indies. For hundreds of years, ships would put in to port here to take on more supplies for their long voyages. Madeiran wine became a sought-after commodity in a remarkably short time after Madeira was claimed by the Portuguese crown in around 1425; by 1450, Madeira was exporting its own wines.

A famous British legend involving Madeira illustrates how early in history it was known in England. It dates from 1478, when the first Duke of Clarence was reportedly executed for treason by being drowned in a butt of Madeira. A butt is a large barrel of about 500 litres. And drowning in his favourite Madeira wine was apparently the duke's own choice.

Legend has it that the Duke of Clarence, after being condemned, chose his own method of execution: drowning in a vat of his beloved Malmsey Madeira.

Gradually, an increasing variety of wine grapes were brought to Madeira from mainland Portugal and other European countries. While Madeira sits at a more southern latitude than the famous wine regions of Europe, its climate is tempered (cooled) by the Atlantic Ocean around it. The grapes grow on the steep slopes of this mountainous island in volcanic soil, which adds to the quality of the wine. In the north, Atlantic winds bring humidity and coolness; on the south side of the mountains there is more sun.

Initially, Madeira wine was made in the same manner as all table wines, but sometime in the 1700s it became the norm to fortify it, which means some neutral grape spirit was added to the wine. Shippers believed this helped stabilize the wine for travel; it also added a welcome element in the form of a higher alcohol level for their customers.

But there's another aspect to this wine: Madeira is unique in that it also benefits from being oxidized – through heating as well as ageing. This was discovered accidentally, apocryphally when wine was taken on a ship through warm ocean waters that heated the barrels. When the wine was sampled later, it was found to have improved so much that winemakers began deliberately shipping their wines around the globe before landing at their final destinations.

Some winemakers also began constructing stoves to heat the rooms in which they aged their wines right on the island, instead of relying solely on warm shipping routes. When the heating process was performed properly, the wines took on a tawny hue, with saline and nutty elements in the aromas and flavours, along with hints of candied and dried fruits ranging from orange marmalade to figs and apricots. And the wine would last forever.

The History of Atlantic Wine

It's curious that a globally significant beverage such as Madeira wine should have originated on a remote island hundreds of kilometres off the coast of the Iberian Peninsula, closer to the continent of Africa than to Europe. Madeira's worth was built by an international cartel

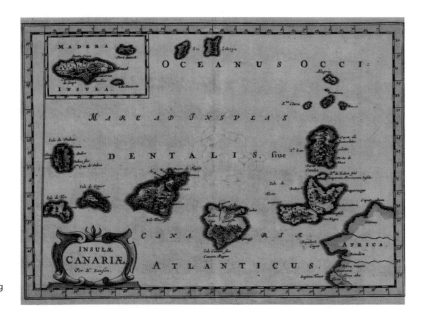

The island of Madeira was well known on shipping routes for hundreds of years even before this 17th-century map was drawn; Madeira was considered an outlying island, like the Canaries.

of merchants, and their customers around the world who craved this wine.

Madeira is a volcanic island sitting out in the Atlantic. With plenty of rainfall on most of the island – and natural water to irrigate the rest – Madeira has a lush appearance, despite its vegetation growing on steep, rocky hillsides. Along the coastline there are a few sandy beaches and many long stretches of cliffs bordering the sea. Above sea level the island is only 741 square kilometres (286 square mi.), smaller than the Greater London Area. Funchal, Madeira's capital, is the only sizeable city; it has a population of over 110,000, and more than one-third of the island's total population lives there.

Madeira was uninhabited when Europeans arrived to colonize it in the early 1400s. Nearby is the island of Porto Santo, which is much smaller than Madeira, and is known mainly as a tourist beach destination today – though it does support some grape-growing and other agriculture. These two, and a few other tiny, uninhabited islands, comprise the Portuguese region of Madeira.

Legend has it that before colonization, two lovers landed on the island in the mid-fourteenth century. It is said that the Englishman Robert Machin (also known as Robert à Machin) was fleeing with the love of his life, Anna d'Arfet, who was a married woman. In their desperation, the couple took to unsafe waters and were driven off course in their boat. Anna apparently did not survive, and Machin was cast up on the shore on the east side of the island we now know as Madeira. The town of Machico is supposedly named after Machin in honour of this romantic tale.

Whether or not this tragic love story occurred, the next significant known date in Madeira's history is 1418, when a trio of seamen landed on Porto Santo while exploring for Prince Henry the Navigator of Portugal. The Madeira islands had appeared on navigation charts since the middle of the 1300s but it took Prince Henry to begin the European colonization of Madeira. He had his father, King João I, appoint one of the trio of 'discoverers', João Gonçalves Zarco, to begin the allotment of lands for settlers. Zarco himself became

the governor of the southwestern part of the island, which included the Funchal area, while his two cohorts divided up the rest; Tristão Vaz Teixera administered the northeastern part of the island of Madeira and Bartolomeu Perestrelo had jurisdiction over the smaller island of Porto Santo.

The three governors were tasked with developing the island as an inhabitable and profitable region for the crown, which imposed taxes on the products of the island. The governors began by attracting foreign investment with incentives to improve land under free leases. When the lands were profitable, they were given or sold to the leaseholders, who were mainly aristocrats – along with a small percentage of wealthy bourgeois merchants and adventurers. The slaves and peasant workers they shipped in, of course, got nothing. This system continued for centuries, with the owners consolidating their lands and inheritances through laws and marriages. In 1863 the system was abolished officially, though its effects continued for another hundred years until after the Portuguese political revolution of 1974, when a more democratic structure was put into place.

The island of Madeira is considered to have a subtropical climate. It has enough rainfall to support inhabitants' drinking-water needs as well as agriculture – when the water is managed, as it has been since the mid-1400s. A *levada* system of channels takes water down the mountains to be used for agricultural irrigation and (originally) for drinking. The *levadas* are still used today, partly for irrigation in agricultural areas, and also in the centre of Funchal and other towns, to try to manage floods caused by torrential rains during the wetter parts of the year.

For centuries, mini-canals called *levadas* have carried critical water from mountain rains throughout the rest of the dry areas of the island of Madeira; this is a particularly beautifully landscaped *levada*.

The traditional *latada* vineyard trellising system keeps the vines secure from ocean winds, and allows other crops to be grown underneath the vines in spring.

Grapes growing in the dry, sandy soil of the nearby island of Porto Santo – the only other place where grapes for Madeira wine can be grown.

Madeira's dramatic, mountainous landscape with its terraced vineyards on the lower hills in the foreground, dormant in winter.

The mountainous centre of the island is so humid that the peaks are often lost in the clouds. The rain is concentrated there and on the northern side of the island. On the mountain tops there may be up to 3,000 mm (120 in.) of average annual rainfall, while the city of Funchal, on the southern coast, has around 550 mm (22 in.).

Those who know the Portuguese language will recognize that the word *madeira* means 'wood'. The island was heavily forested when the first settlers arrived from Europe. It was the landowners who, early on, burned the luxuriant forests of Madeira in order to open up land for agriculture. Wood ash also enriches the land, so this was not an entirely negative action; in fact it was considered an improvement at the time. In addition to grapes, farming entrepreneurs also planted sugar cane, which became one of the major exports of Madeira in the fifteenth century. Explorer Christopher Columbus came to the

Madeira islands to learn about the sugar trade before his voyages of discovery to the Americas. He lived there for a few years, and married the daughter of Perestrelo, the first governor of the island of Porto Santo. A house Columbus built later still stands in Porto Santo, and is now a museum.

Sugar had always been scarce in Europe, and Madeira's sugar cane became such a desirable export that it quickly dwarfed everything else. At this time it was common to import slaves from African and Arab nations to work the land, and, tragically, this is what occurred here. Sugar cane practically became a monoculture. In a relatively short time this led to famine and other drastic consequences, first when the land was overcultivated, and then when the West Indies and Brazil became much larger and cheaper sources for sugar, which happened by the mid-seventeenth century.

A system whereby foreigners controlled a significant part of Madeira's commerce and agriculture had been established early on. The first residents of Madeira were aristocrats from the Portuguese mainland, followed by Italian, Flemish, French and Spanish Castilian nobility, with a small percentage of British and other wealthy bourgeois who were willing to take the risk of making a profit – and a life for themselves – on this unknown island. They were encouraged by the first successful sugar plantations; initially they also exported some grain and wood. The export market was founded on a system of taxes and fees, and in this area the Italians first dominated with their banking experience.

Additionally, from the beginning, the new Madeiran oligarchy grew grapes and made wine, employing mainly Portuguese peasants to work the vineyards. The vineyards were small, carved out of formerly wooded land, often on steep hills that inspired the creation of endless terraces (*poios*) throughout the island. There is more than one reason for this. Under a covenant that applied to Madeira's early landowners, a contract referred to as *bemfeitorias* was put into place. Essentially, a landowner could seize back any of his land worked by peasant farmers – but only if the landowner compensated the farmer for all the improvements (*bemfeitorias*) the farmer had put into the land. Because it was usually too costly to pay for all the terracing work, the farmers who built walls and other amendments on their small plots were basically assured of their tenure on the land. Of course, the farmers were obliged to 'sell' a large percentage of their grapes (and other crops) to the landowners. The landowners controlled the distribution, and eventually the export, of finished, aged wines, but this system did offer a measure of security by enabling the peasants to provide food for their own families.

After the Anglo-Portuguese treaty of 1654, more British merchants went to Madeira to source wine for export. (They also went to Oporto at this time, which was the beginning of the meteoric rise of the port industry.) The first British 'factory' or association of merchants on Madeira dates to around 1658. This period also coincided with the beginning of European colonization of the New World as well as Africa, India and what was then called the Far East, all of which were soon to become rapidly growing new markets for wine as well as for manufactured goods from Britain and Europe.

But Madeira had an added geographical asset, being strategically located out in the southern Atlantic, where winds and ocean currents formed trade routes both to the New World and to Asia. Many ships stopped here for provisions that included wine for their crews as well as for commerce. Because people liked the taste of Madeira, and because the wine travelled well, Madeira was one of the few globally available wines for several centuries.

In the seventeenth century, Brazil, a Portuguese colony, had become the largest export market for Madeira wine, but this market started to decline after colonists' preference switched to port. However, during that period, importing Madeira wine became – and remained – important in many other areas of the globe because many of the colonies of Portugal, Britain and other countries were situated in regions that were too warm to grow wine grapes (*Vitis vinifera*).

In North America, the climate of the early colonies was not hospitable to *Vitis vinifera*, which was not native to that continent.

Native North American grapes proved unsatisfactory for making wine in the temperate areas, and initially there was no local large source of grain or sugar to create other forms of alcohol along the East Coast. Imported wines were in demand throughout America from the early 1700s, essential in the homes of cultured and successful families. Wine was expensive, though, because it was taxed by Britain on the way to America on British ships.

Once again, Madeira's location proved providential when in 1660 this island was granted exemption from the law that required only British ships from British ports to take goods to America. In all probability, the earlier law was proving unenforceable on an island so far out in the middle of the ocean. However, the wine was still taxable upon arrival in the colonies, an issue that was to prove significant in pre-Revolutionary times in America.

The number of Madeira shippers grew rapidly, and the Portuguese and British were soon joined by shippers from a variety of countries, including North America, Denmark, the Netherlands, France, Italy and Spain. During that century, the export of wine was overtaking that of sugar in volume and value. By 1768, just before the American War of Independence, wine was the primary export, and there were over two hundred Madeira shippers, the lion's share being small Portuguese companies. However, the largest shippers were British or American. Records of some of these exporters show that at first they essentially divided up the territories of the world, while later in the century they competed for customers. All together, firms shipped Madeira wine to England, Scotland, Ireland, the Netherlands, Spain, Portugal, Canada, the American territories (states), Jamaica, Barbados and other parts of the West Indies, Africa, India and Asia.

During the years leading up to the United States Declaration of Independence in 1776, Madeira had been embraced by the colonists who were eager to be out from under British taxation because Madeira wine could often be taken aboard American colonists' ships and unloaded in discreet ports, evading British tax inspectors. But not always. Some years before the American Revolution began, a conflict involving Madeira wine escalated ill feelings between the colonists and the British rulers. It took place aboard the sloop *Liberty*, owned by John Hancock, whose signature is the most prominent on the Declaration of Independence.

In 1768 Hancock had brought in perhaps a hundred pipes of Madeira wine, and in such instances His Majesty's custom officials habitually taxed only a portion of the cargo. This time, the British governors were clamping down, so the agent came aboard and insisted on Hancock paying taxes for the entire amount – with the taxes going to support Britain. This was a key item in the colonists' revolt: they felt they were being subjected to 'taxation without representation'. In other words, the Americans paid the crown but had no representatives in the British government.

As it's told, Hancock took the customs agent prisoner while he offloaded most of the Madeira, so there was only a small portion of the wine left when the customs agent was set free to examine the cargo. But the story got out. The British took their revenge by seizing the *Liberty* from Hancock and using it as a British patrol ship on nearby waters. This only added fire to Hancock's determination to free his country from British overseers.

The Declaration of Independence is said to have been toasted by its authors and signatories – the elite of the American political rebellion – with Madeira wine. Very possibly this was the American favourite rainwater Madeira, which was most well known along the southern section of the u.s. east coast. From the late 1700s until the turn of the twentieth century, Madeira was the gentlemen's drink of choice at home and in private clubs from Baltimore to Savannah; there is still a residual pro-Madeira culture in the latter and in Charleston, South Carolina. Rainwater is a slightly lighter-coloured Madeira, long-ageing and not dilute, despite its name. There are legends about its creation involving rainwater literally falling into an open barrel of wine on a ship, on a beach, or in a city such as Charleston or Savannah. Whatever the truth, this style of Madeira is inextricably linked with American history and patriotism.

In both Britain and in America, during the eighteenth century drinking Madeira was a sign of prosperity and gentility, too; it was a requirement in society, and the Madeira wine industry kept booming. American independence leaders Thomas Jefferson and George Washington were great aficionados of Madeira. In fact, in the last decades of the century, between a third and half of Madeira's total wine exports went to the port of New York.

Sadly, Madeira's great success in the world also created the circumstances for its disgrace soon afterwards. A worldwide increase in demand for Madeira meant consumer demand for a consistent and high-quality product. Shippers with offices in Funchal (the capital city) were in control of the wine. But without the instant communication methods we have today, news took weeks or months to travel to and from Madeira. So when Madeira's rise in the world started spawning a number of imitators – sellers of fraudulent Madeira – it took a long time for the real producers to become aware of this. And in a British-dominated world of commerce, it may have taken even longer for those who were brought up on the honour system to begin to act against the counterfeiters. Whatever they did, it was too little, too late.

Even on the island of Madeira, in the late eighteenth and early nineteenth centuries Madeira producers had been having trouble with consistency and quantities in the effort to meet growing demand for their wines. Some of the winemakers new to the special method of heating the wine overdid it, and the wines came out with toasted or cooked flavours. So much so that some of the counterfeit Madeiras (the adulterated or badly replicated wines from other countries) did not seem much different from the poorly made Madeira-originated wines of the time.

Trade had already been fairly volatile in several regions beginning in the late eighteenth century, as for example when the American market dried up during the War of Independence (1775–83). Following that, the French Revolution and the Napoleonic Wars wreaked havoc on the British wine trade with France, so the

Madeira trade flourished for a time until the French wines were available again.

There is another famous Madeira story, this one involving Napoleon – and Winston Churchill. According to a legend told by the Blandy family (important Madeira shippers since 1811), Napoleon stopped in Madeira in 1815 on his way to his final exile on the remote South Atlantic island of St Helena. One of the supplies that Napoleon's retinue picked up was a barrel of Madeira dating from 1792. After Napoleon died in 1820, the barrel was found unopened, and since it had not been paid for, the original shipping merchant retrieved it and sold it back to the Blandys. This fine Madeira was considered to be barely old enough to be drinkable even then, so they left it to age for a while longer. It was bottled in 1840, and the bottles were doled out very sparingly. It is said that Winston Churchill drank one of the last bottles when he visited Madeira in 1950. It is also said that this legend is pure fabrication. Very likely Napoleon had nothing to do with any Blandy 1792/1840 Madeira. Perhaps the year 1792 is significant because it was the date of the beginning of a famous Blandy Madeira solera. This solera was real, and so legendary that the last of it was finally bottled for a state visit of Queen Elizabeth II in 1957. However, enduring tales like these linking Madeira with historical luminaries like Napoleon, Churchill and Queen Elizabeth do serve to illustrate Madeira's lasting sovereign status.

Returning to the nineteenth century, in 1852 the dreaded grapevine plague oidium hit the island, decimating the vineyards. Eventually a remedy (sulphur) was discovered, though it took some time for this to be applied and for vineyard health to resume. In the 1860s the u.s. Madeira trade ground to a halt once again, during the American Civil War, and it never really recovered. However, there continued to be a substantial market for Madeira in India, the uk, Germany and Russia.

Then in 1872 the fatal phylloxera vine plague arrived in Madeira from America via the uk and/or Europe, and it took ten years for a solution to be proved – and used – on the island. Because this

Blandy's treasured storehouse of aged Madeira wines: after decades in barrel, when Madeira wine reaches the limit of its ageability in wood, it is transfered into small glass containers.

involved planting new roots and grafting the vines, further years were necessary to grow new grapevines to an age where they produced viable grapes to make wine. During both of these vine diseases, there were many attempts to make Madeira with all sorts of grapes and techniques, and the results did Madeira's reputation no favours.

Madeira wine exports rose again during the end of the nineteenth century and the beginning of the twentieth. However, the First and Second World Wars drastically disrupted trade. The Russian Revolution of 1917 destroyed another lucrative market for Madeira. In the U.S., Prohibition (1920–33) was the final death knell for Madeira's lustre in that country. The British market did recover between the wars, however, and there were additional great increases in exports of Madeira to Switzerland, Germany and Scandinavia.

From 1924 to 1974, Portugal as a country was essentially sequestered under a totalitarian government that had its own plans for the island of Madeira. Looking at the declining exports of wine in both volume and value, the regime encouraged Madeirans to plant bananas and other tropical fruits. This proved to be a great strategy for fruit growing, but at the expense of grape growing. Further, many grape growers were subsidized to re-graft their traditional grapes to international varieties (not usable for Madeira wine) in order to

produce more widely known wine styles. It would be many more decades before the world at large began to rediscover Madeira: both the island and its wine.

A Forever Wine

Madeira wine is one of the easiest wines in the world to store – in fact it is probably *the* easiest wine to store. And buying it is fairly simple, too, because it's nearly impossible to find a wine that has been damaged while being stored. The main thing to remember is to buy from a reputable wine purveyor.

Because of the relative scarcity and low demand for Madeira wine at present, there is little danger of purchasing a recent counterfeit wine. Without being an expert, leakage and low fill levels in bottles (ullage) are two elements any consumer can question when purchasing very old wines. However, most wine sellers and auction houses are especially careful these days, having learned caution from recent highly publicized reports of historic wine forgeries.

If there are less-than-honestly-labelled Madeira wines for sale today, it is likely that they came on the market in the second half

Older Madeira wines are found on the shelves of wine shops today because Madeira lasts for decades, even a century or more.

Barrels of Blandy's Madeira patiently ageing in their attic warehouse in the centre of the city of Funchal.

of the twentieth century. This is when Madeira wine was declining in importance, when fewer consumers had any knowledge about the wine and when young travellers were just starting to rediscover 'out-of-the-way' islands like Madeira. Opportunistic shops on the island (and elsewhere) could have taken advantage of wide-eyed innocent tourists. Not every bottle of wine purchased by a 'rediscoverer' of Madeira is a problem, but that is where issues can occur – often only coming to light when a relative's wine cellar is sold by the owner's heirs. Some research into Madeira can be done online, but consulting one of the larger auction houses may be the simplest way to get an evaluation of an old Madeira wine.

The operative word here is 'old', even 'very old'. Madeira has a (well-deserved) reputation as the world's oldest consumable wine. But even Madeira only lives for so long. And the number of bottles of historic Madeira is limited. In the past there have been unsubstantiated historic Madeira bottles purchased and repurchased by collectors.

Because instant communication makes transparency the norm nowadays, it is now possible for an ordinary wine consumer to purchase a well-verified bottle of fifty- or hundred-year-old Madeira, either on the island or from an importer in their home country. In terms of price, it will be relatively reasonable – especially for a wine of its age. A reputably purchased Madeira, one can be assured, will be wonderful to drink at fifty or more years of age.

One of the ways Madeira wine producers handle their extremely ageable wine is to bottle as necessary when stocks of the older wines are running low. And they now indicate the bottling date on the label. While Madeira wines age in casks, at a certain point the wines do achieve maximum barrel age. Experienced cellar-masters know when this moment has arrived. Some of the wine will be bottled and the remainder will be sealed in glass containers so there will be no further oxidation or evaporation. Labels will be affixed to the retail bottles that include the bottling date. This is a date that the company is proud of because it shows the extent of their old stocks. So the bottling date should be easily visible, often on the back label.

The conventional wisdom with wines is that over 95 per cent of wine purchased today is meant to be consumed within a year or two of purchase. With Madeira, this is also true: the wines available at wine shops are also ready to drink. All the ageing required for Madeira wine is accomplished before the wines are shipped out. However, if a bottle is forgotten at the back of a closet or the bottom of a wine cellar, there's no need for despair. The overwhelming chances are that the Madeira will still be good even decades after it is purchased. This is especially true of the higher grades of Madeira wines.

Madeira wine is typically served in small glasses, with a serving being around half that of a table wine. The character of Madeira demands that it be paid attention to, from the complex aromas to the opulent flavours in each sip. Traditionally, drier Madeiras could be served before the meal, and sweeter ones afterwards. But because Madeira wines are so rich, these days most people tend to serve them at the end of the meal, either with a cheese course or with sweets.

Madeira wines are exceptional in that they can actually complement robust desserts: the sweeter Madeiras possess the combination of body, flavours, acidity and sweetness that can stand up to many dessert dishes, whether their preparation involves chocolate, nuts, cream or fruit.

Then there is the famous Madeira cake, traditionally served as a late morning snack or at tea time. The cake became well known not because Madeira wine is an ingredient, but because it is the perfect accompaniment to the wine; it is a flavourful, round, single-layer cake made with local, sugar-cane 'honey', almonds and spices. This rich cake is still made on the island today, most typically in the late autumn for people to enjoy over the December holidays, and through the winter. And many British families have their own tried-and-true Madeira cake recipes.

Grapes

Most of the grapes used in Madeira were brought from northern Portugal, notably the four major original grapes used to make this wine: Sercial (also known as Esgana Cão), Verdelho (also known as Verdello), Boal (also known as Bual) and Malvasia (also spelled Malvazia).

The lion's share of Malvasia currently used in Madeira wine production is Malvasia de São Jorge. A much smaller amount of another Malvasia is also used: Malvasia Candida, which is sometimes referred to as Malvasia Candia. This is actually Malvasia di Candia, one of the most notable, ancient versions of the grape. It most likely originated in Candia (now called Heraklion), the capital of Crete, though the grape had made its way across the Mediterranean to be planted in several other countries by the time it was transplanted to Madeira. Malvasia has held an exalted position for centuries; since Grecian times, many different fine wines have been called 'Malvasia' (or a variant of this name in other languages). There is also a rare red version called Malvasia Candida Roxa.

Historically, Madeira wines made with Malvasia grapes were considered to be the finest because these grapes produce a wine that is complex and delicate; it is the sweetest of all the Madeiras yet somehow carries an undercurrent of savouriness. Also, it is important to remember that, in the world of Madeira, Malvasia wine is known as 'malmsey', a centuries-old contraction of the word 'Malvasia'. To further confuse matters, it is thought that the grape known in Madeira as Boal is actually the grape known in other places as 'Malvasia Fina' – though that name is not used on the island of Madeira.

Over the course of the past several centuries, additional white and red grapes have been used to make Madeira wine, both unofficially and officially. As recently as a few years ago (and for many decades before that), various grapes were used to enhance the wine's colour and flavour, and/or reduce production costs. But there is a

One of the less well-known Madeira wine grapes, Malvasia de São Jorge, growing on a steep hillside in a traditional, *latada*-trellised vineyard.

Long bunches of Bual (Boal) grapes, close to harvest time, in Justino's vineyards.

Small, plump bunches of Terrantez grapes on the vine in the Justino's wine company vineyards.

These Bastardo grapes are notoriously difficult to grow, but they are making a comeback in fine Madeira wines today.

system in place now. Once a grape variety has been officially 'recognized' as used in Madeira wine production, it enters a list as 'allowed'. Later, some grapes are elevated to 'recommended' status. Only recommended grapes can be highlighted on a Madeira wine label.

Current 'authorized' grapes are Caracol, which is grown on Porto Santo, Complexa (which is gaining in popularity), Deliciosa, Rio-Grande, Triunfo and Valveirinho. Additional recommended grapes for Madeira wine include Bastardo, also known as Graciosa, or as Trousseau Noir in other countries; Folgasão, also known as Terrantez (and which has nothing to do with the Spanish grape Torrontes); Listrão, which is grown only on the island of Porto Santo; Moscatel Graudo, also known as Moscatel de Setúbal; Tinta; Tinta-Negra, also known as Molar or Saborinho; and Verdelho Tinto.

Bastardo is the most in-demand grape right now, partly owing to its scarcity and partly because Barabeito, one of the trendiest producers, has secured a tiny allotment of this grape to make Madeira wine. The grape is very hard to grow; it needs a lot of care and produces very low yields. In the past, say fifty or a hundred years ago (or more), Bastardo was more widely grown, so other producers now can occasionally make available old Madeira wines that were made with this grape.

Tinta Negra is the new favourite workhorse of the Madeira producers. It is estimated that 90 per cent of the Madeira wine grapes now grown on the island are Tinta Negra. Madeira has traditionally been made with white grapes, but the red Tinta Negra is so easy to grow and produces such a hearty and authentic-style Madeira wine when young that its use is wildly increasing. Nearly all of the Madeira that is made to be sold young (the three-year-old wine) is now being made with the Tinta Negra grape. As of 2015, Tinta Negra transitioned from the grey area of being 'allowed' into being an official grape for Madeira wine production. Tinta Negra can be made into wines in all four Madeiran categories of sweetness.

Madeira Production

For hundreds of years, Madeira wine was produced under the auspices of the shippers of Madeira. Thousands of small growers harvested their own grapes, then conveyed them to large wineries, where they were paid for their crop. The more the grapes weighed, the more the farmers were paid – until recent decades when more stringent measures were put into place, and quality has become favoured over quantity. For the first time, farmers are now being turned away if their grapes do not live up to the specifications of the wine producers. If this happens more than once or twice, the farmer may be banned even from trying to sell his grapes to the winery, which is a rare phenomenon, but does happen. All grapes for Madeira wine are hand-harvested, owing to the rough topography of the island and the small sizes of the individual farmers' plots.

The Madeira wine producers have remained dependent on small farmers because the producers generally do not own vineyards themselves. Only a couple of the major producers own some vineyards: Henriques & Henriques and the Madeira Wine Company.

At the wineries, the grapes are pressed and fermented according to the optimal method for each variety. Until the mid-eighteenth century, most of Madeira's wines were fermented dry, placed into wooden barrels and sold that way. Madeira wines are always aged in 'neutral' wooden vats and barrels, so the character of the wood is not a major factor in the finished wines. But during the course of the 1600s and early 1700s, two interesting phenomena were discovered and codified: the effects of alcohol being added to the wine during fermentation; and the effects of heat on the fermented wine afterward.

It was discovered that Madeira wines were more resilient, more immune to the rigours of travel by ship, if they were fortified. Originally, the spirit was added to the barrels just before shipping. Eventually, through trial and error, it was discovered that Madeira wines tasted best – and shipped well – when the spirit was added

The perennially difficult grape harvest in nearly vertical vineyards on Madeira.

to the wine near the end of the fermentation process, but before the fermentation was completed. Fortification shuts down the fermentation process by creating an environment that has too much alcohol for the yeast to exist. The result is that some of the natural sweetness of the grapes does not get converted to alcohol by the yeast, and remains in the finished wine.

Oxidation and heat are generally the enemies of table wine but instead of ruining Madeira wines, these elements improve its ageing, its aromas and its complex flavours. At first, this was accidental. Now it is deliberate, because both of these processes have been found to be essential in creating great Madeiras.

Wine oxidizes when air remains in the wine barrels because they are not quite filled with wine and also because of evaporation, which is especially rapid in a warm climate. The result is a layer of air at the top of the barrel, so oxygen interacts with the surface of the wine. In addition, oxygen from the environment may slowly penetrate the wood from outside. (The barrel's wood also contributes to the finished colour of the wine.)

Heat, which is the enemy of most table wines, is also required in order to produce great Madeira wine. Historically, casks were sometimes stored in warm places while ageing, and they also experienced warm temperatures during transportation through warm seas to customers abroad. Whatever the cause, this seemed to improve the wine in its early years, and also to contribute markedly to the wine's ageability.

This was discovered accidentally because Madeira wines started off in the warm South Atlantic and were shipped to many warm-climate ports and occasionally, full Madeira wine barrels would end up returning to Madeira. Perhaps the barrels were more valuable to the ship's captain as ballast; perhaps they were forgotten or remained unsold abroad. In any case, after the movement of the ocean and the heat of the voyage, curiously, the Madeira wines always improved. They became more complex, exhibiting the character of a longer-aged wine in a much shorter amount of time.

The improvement was so great that shippers began deliberately sending Madeira barrels on longer trips before their final destination, or even on round trips where, upon their return, the wines were found to be of an even higher quality, making them much more valuable. These very desirable wines were termed *Vinho Madeira Torna-Viagem* or *Vinho da Roda*. Even today, barrels are occasionally sent on ocean voyages and returned to Madeira, which makes them develop more quickly, adding complexity as well as prestige and value. This is more of a promotional variation in production because it is such a rare (and somewhat costly) occurrence. But it apparently does improve the wine – often more rapidly than conventional ageing in Madeira. (The effect of motion on Madeira wine has not been studied fully; at present this element is not thought to contribute greatly to the development of the wine.)

To return to the issue of heat, in the late 1700s, in order to provide consistent, higher-quality wines, Madeira winemakers began deliberately heating their wines while they were in barrels. They built little stoves to place in their wine storage rooms, and heated them for weeks and months. This method is known as *estufagem* and has been used ever since, for varying lengths of time, and at varying temperatures; now it is all controlled electronically.

The other style of ageing Madeira with heat uses the natural heat of the climate. It is called *canteiro* because the barrels were placed on the top floors of houses or warehouses, on wooden beams that are called *canteiros*, in order to take advantage of the highest natural temperatures in the building. The *canteiro* process is also used today, with wine barrels placed in uninsulated rooms, or even by sunny windows.

Though the specifications and names for Madeira wine styles have changed over time, the most recent regulations took effect only recently, in 2015. These guidelines and parameters have been created based on the latest production methods and consumption trends. Today, according to regulation, though Madeira may be heated up to 50°C (122°F), the best winemakers agree that a maximum temperature of 45°C (113°F) is optimum. Heating methods have changed over the decades. When metal tanks were introduced into the winemaking process in the twentieth century, some winemakers used internal heating elements in various shapes. But these were found to heat the wine unevenly, so the latest iterations locate the heating elements on the outsides of the tanks. Still, winemakers may have to stir the wine within in order to ensure even heating. Best practices now call for the wines to be heated for a period of three to four months. Currently, the youngest (three-year) Madeiras are all produced this way, with some of the other styles made by the *canteiro* or partial-*canteiro* method.

By far the largest percentage of young Madeira wines are used in culinary preparations around the globe. In order to distinguish between culinary and drinking Madeiras, many of the culinary-use Madeiras are laced with salt and sometimes pepper too. These spices are fine when the Madeira wines are used in sauces, but would be a disaster in a wine glass. This practice is intended to prevent fraud; so, for example, an unscrupulous importer would not be able to import bulk Madeira cheaply, then bottle it for profit as a beverage in another country.

Madeira wine categories are defined by Baumé (density) measurements, not by residual sugar, though there are approximate correlations: dry = 0–1.5° Baumé (roughly 0–55 grams/litre); medium dry = 1.5°–2.5° Baumé (about 55–75 g/l); medium sweet = 2.5°–3.5° Baumé (about 75–95 g/l); and sweet = more than 3.5° Baumé (over 95 g/l). There is also a rare, extra dry category of 0.5° Baumé or less.

The Madeira wine vineyard areas are strictly demarcated on both Madeira and Porto Santo, the only regions where Madeira wine can be made. Madeira vineyard and wine regulations are overseen by a government body which has undergone several name changes since its inception in 1979. In 2006 Madeira's renowned artisanal embroidery and artisanal products were added to the purvue of this bureau, and it is now referred to as IVBAM, which stands for Instituto do Vinho, do Bordado e do Artesano da Madeira.

Fortification is regulated by IVBAM rules. Protected Designation of Origin (DOP) Madeira must have a finished alcohol content of 17–22 per cent. Finished Madeira wines traditionally come in at 18–19 per cent. Madeira wines can be dry, medium dry, medium sweet or sweet, depending on when the fermentation process is stopped by fortification. (Note that DOP is the same as PDO; both are updates of the older EU term 'Controlled Designation of Origin', often abbreviated to DO or DOC.)

The alcohol used for fortification must be distilled from grapes. And it must be a neutral, pure (96 per cent) alcohol. IVBAM also supports grape growers with information and advice from their staff viticulturist. At present, one of the viticulturist's challenges is trying to get small growers to change their almost superstitious dependence on growing grapes in the traditional, very low canopy style called *latadas*. In some places the canopy is barely a metre high (a little over a yard) to guard against damage from severe windstorms on the north side of the island. It was also traditional for the farmers to plant vegetables under the canopies either before or after the grape harvest. In some areas this continues, and modern viticulturalists believe *latadas* can be problematic for clean grape-growing and harvesting conditions.

Wine Styles

Formerly, all Madeira was known by the name of the grape it was made from, and it's important to know that each grape name also indicated the amount of sweetness in the wine. Wines can also be labelled with a specific indicator of the 'richness' of the wine; different conventions apply in different countries. There were also some special names used in different regions, like 'London Particular', which was bottled for the UK market. (Incidentally, this name was also used for a style of Marsala.) In addition, natural caramel colour may be added to Madeira. This was historically used to accommodate differing customer preferences in various regions of the world.

In terms of styles, Madeira labels use names involving the terms 'dry' and 'rich' to denote the relative dryness and sweetness of the wines. In the past there were four major grapes that were made into Madeira wines. Sercial grapes made the 'dry' (driest) wines. The grape name Verdelho indicated the wine was 'medium dry'. Bual grapes made a medium sweet wine, which was also called 'medium rich'. Lastly, malmsey, an early contraction of 'Malvasia' specific to Madeira, was the sweetest wine; it was also called 'rich Madeira'. Today, in order for a wine to be labelled by its grape name, the wine must contain at least 85 per cent of that grape.

There are two additional labelling denominations: single vintage and defined age. Interestingly, the age of a Madeira is officially sanctioned only organoleptically, by a panel of experts. Apparently, Madeira producers had wanted to use the designation 'vintage' for single-vintage wines, but in Portugal it was felt that the term 'vintage' (in English) somehow belonged to the producers of port wine.

Age-defined colheita wines are labelled with a harvest date; they must be aged in wood for at least five years, and must exhibit defined organoleptic characteristics. The term *frasqueira* is used for exceptional wines that have been aged for twenty years in wood, in the *canteiro* system; these are most often single-grape and single-vintage wines.

Blended Madeiras that are a minimum of five years old may also be labelled 'Reserve'. Those that are ten years old may be called 'Old Reserve' (or 'Special Reserve' or 'Very Old'). A tasting panel organoleptically evaluates samples in these higher categories of wines before they can officially be labelled. Older wines must be evaluated for their typicity before being labelled fifteen-year-old (or 'Extra Reserve') or twenty-, thirty- or over-forty-year-old wines (which may also carry the designation 'Selected', 'Choice', or 'Finest'). A perfectly balanced wine may be labelled 'Fine'.

These glasses indicate the correct colours of the different styles of Madeira wines.

Some wines are made with the solera method (like sherry). In this case, no more than 10 per cent of an older wine in barrels can be removed for blending and/or bottling, and it must be replaced with a younger wine of equal quality; this addition may be performed up to ten times, after which all the wine in the solera must be bottled. These wines are labelled with the harvest year of the solera's base wine.

The term 'rainwater Madeira' now refers to a fairly young Madeira, with at least three and less than ten years of ageing. Currently, it is most often made with Tinta Negra grapes. It is the only Madeira where colour is strictly determined; it must be pale, and within certain guidelines of lightness. One way this can be accomplished is by de-stemming the grapes before a very light pressing. Rainwater Madeira can be enjoyed both before and after the meal; it is primarily consumed in the u.s., which has a long tradition of imbibing this wine.

Companies, Contraction and Consolidation

One of the most famous wine writers of the early twentieth century was the British writer George Saintsbury. He was primarily a historian but his well-regarded publications on wine prove that he was much more than an 'amateur' wine lover – as he probably would have characterized himself in print. His famous *Notes on a Cellar-book* went into multiple printings in 1920, the first year it was published.

Yet even a hundred years ago, Saintsbury was lamenting the 'good old days' of wine. First he declared his esteem for Madeira, avowing: 'I know of no wine of its class that can beat Madeira when at its best . . . In fact I think Madeira and Burgundy carry combined intensity and complexity of vinous delights further than any other wines.' Yet he also cautions readers:

> I fear that the very best Madeira is, and always has been since
> the pre-oidium wines were exhausted, mainly a memory. I had
> some of these . . . when my cellar-book started, but I seldom

cared to replace them with their degenerate successors . . . I have
drunk 1780 Madeira when it was nearly ninety years old and in
perfection [which] was a thing to say grace for and remember.

Cultural changes during the twentieth century contributed to the
decline in Madeira consumption. Many of those who had enjoyed
Madeira were no longer living the same aristocratic lifestyle owing
to socio-political changes in the world. Added to this was the physical decline in family-owned Madeira firms: the traditional British
shipping families began to die out or diversify because the companies
could not sustain them. By the mid-twentieth century this landscape
had irrevocably contracted.

Portugal joined the European Community in 1986, and soon
began to receive its support. The EC (now called the EU) clearly
placed a great deal of value on its members' cultural histories. In
1992 Madeira winemakers first received critical grants from the
Programa de Opções Específicas para fazer face ao Afastamento
e á Insularidade da Madiera e dos Açores (Programme of Specific
Options to deal with the Remoteness and Insularity of Madeira and
the Azores, or POSEIMA). These programmes have been renewed
every five years, and they have kept a great deal of the Madeira wine
industry alive. In essence, they subsidize the companies to continue
to age their wines as tradition and regulation dictate – a practice that
ties up a substantial amount of capital in wine stocks for many years.
Most wineries have official 'POSEI' inspection seals on a number of
their barrels, clearly visible in the ageing rooms.

One more major change in Madeira wine shipping regulations
was put into place at the beginning of this century. As of the year
2002, all Madeira wines are required to be bottled on the island.
(Culinary Madeiras can be shipped in bulk, but as noted earlier,
they are often adulterated with salt and even pepper so they cannot
be bottled elsewhere and sold for drinking.)

Over the past hundred years, Madeira shipping companies have
been forced to consolidate and consolidate and consolidate again.

In 1925 the Madeira Wine Association was formed by the prominent Blandy and Leacock companies. A new association with the same name was formed in 1934, adding more companies to the roster, and this continued for decades, until the company had absorbed the famed Cossart, Gordon & Co., along with more than a dozen well-known and lesser-known shippers. For economies of scale, all the companies pooled their stocks from the time they joined – though small, individual amounts of old soleras or vintage wines were maintained by the original companies. The wines to be bottled were blended centrally, though they were separated along the lines of each company's style. Each company had its own labels for the new wines, but all commerce and trading was performed by the central body.

Eventually, the Blandy company took control of the Madeira Wine Association. In 1989 they brought in the distinguished Symington family, which had been amalgamating port companies in order to maintain and expand port's eminence and value during its lean times. The Symington alliance lasted for twenty years, but eventually they stepped out and the Blandy group took over the company once again – this time renaming it Blandy's.

Sixty Madeira shippers had been registered to trade at the time of the Second World War. Each successive decade has seen a further decline in numbers. At the time of this writing there were only eight remaining Madeira companies exporting from Funchal to many countries around the globe, some of which are traditional, centuries-old markets, and some of which are very new or revitalized regions.

Yet somehow the eight are not only surviving, but learning new ways to brand themselves and their wines. Blandy's, for example, has become the headquarters for Madeira wine tourism, with their tours, ageing rooms, tasting rooms and a restaurant located in the heart of Funchal. Eager sightseers form a continuous stream into this warren of picturesque buildings – buildings which once housed a Franciscan monastery, a hospital, a prison and a courthouse. Here, Blandy's maintain stores of older wines (though the company also

Display of Madeira
wines and other island
products in the delightfully
traditional tasting room at
the Pereira d'Oliveira wine
company in Funchal.

continues to produce new Madeiras each year) and visitors lap up
the traditions and the family lore along with the wines.

In addition to Blandy's, the Cossart & Gordon and Miles lines
of Madeira are based here in the same buildings. They are in the
business not only of educating tourists at their facility, but of creating
new, loyal consumers for their wines. On wine labels, these Madeira
companies now include the numbers of casks and bottles produced,
dates of bottling and other interesting details. They are also target-
ing mixologists and cocktail lovers at their annual wine festival,

using their three-year-old 'Duke of Clarence' and their five-year-old 'Alvada' Madeiras as bases for a cocktail competition.

Another historic producer, Pereira d'Oliveira, is also a charming place to visit, fulfilling one's vision of Madeira's past with its unrestrained, wonderfully retro-style decor. The tasting room is large, with tables and chairs and infinite historic and modern Madeira-related objects to examine on shelves and on the walls. Visitors there can purchase everything from stocks of Madeira cake (in autumn and winter) to wine books and maps of the island – and, of course, the wines, which include new bottlings of very old Madeiras.

Pereira D'Oliveira now encompasses six formerly separate Madeira companies, and is run by the polished and gentlemanly Luis A. C. D'Oliveira, along with a brother who resides in Lisbon. They are fifth-generation family members, and a nephew is currently in training as a winemaker.

Mr D'Oliveira's great-grandfather's eponymous company was founded in 1850. It later merged with João Joaquim Camacho Sucessores (founded in 1870). Until the 1980s, the company sold their wines locally and on mainland Portugal. The D'Oliveira family achieved some of their success by selling wine to tourists who visited on cruise ships; maritime tourism here is a two-hundred-year-old tradition, according to Mr D'Oliveira. Several other companies have also been acquired in past consolidations: in 1953, Júlio Augusta Cunha and Sons (founded in 1820); in 1983, Vasco Luis Pereira and Sons (founded in 1890); in 2001, they acquired Adegas do Torreão (Vinhos), Lda. (established 1949); and in 2013, they also took over Artur Barros e Sousa, Lda. (founded in 1921).

With all this consolidation, Mr D'Oliveira explains that their stocks of old wines are so vast that they don't need to produce large quantities of wine now. However, each year they do continue to buy grapes from the same 90–110 families. Every year they dig deep into their treasures and bottle both newer and older wines. In 2018, for example, they released a sweet 2005 'Malvazia' and a 1998 Tinta

Negra, a medium-sweet 1998 Boal and a medium-dry 1978 Terrantez. They now add bottling dates to their labels. They own quite a bit of rare wine in excellent condition, including, for example, a 1927 vintage Bastardo, a Verdelho from 1932 which was last bottled in 2011, a 1907 'Reserva' Malvasia bottled in 2003 (in a squashed-looking bottle as a fun tribute to its age) and an award-winning 1908 Boal which has been bottled periodically, most recently in 2016.

Another family-owned company, H. M. Borges, was established in 1877 and is now run by two fourth-generation cousins, Helena and Isabel Borges. They make quite a bit of their Madeira with Tinta Negra because they appreciate that it has good productivity and acidity; they like it because the grape is versatile, develops faster and produces a lighter wine. They also use some Brazilian *setin* (satinwood) barrels for ageing. In common with other producers, they add bottling dates to the labels of their older wines.

H. M. Borges exports 80 per cent of its wines. Their older markets are Norway and Sweden – and Japan for the medium-sweet style, since the 1950s. Russia is now starting to import their wines, as are Belgium, the UK and Italy. Their tasting room in Funchal is in a historic building: a former flour mill which the family acquired in the 1920s.

The prominent firm of Henriques & Henriques was established in 1850. The last surviving member of the family died in 1968 and the company was left to three of his friends; today the company is run by Humberto Jardim, the son of one of the three. He took over the helm of the company when it was moving its winemaking production out of the original company headquarters in the seaside fishing village of Câmara de Lobos. After renovating the original building, Henriques & Henriques created a public tasting area and shop, and several floors of visually appealing barrel-ageing rooms. The financial stresses on the company were crippling, but luckily Jardim forged a timely deal with La Martiniquaise, a spirits conglomerate that had already purchased another Madeira wine company called Justino's.

Justino's vineyards, with a rushing stream in historic *levadas* that channel the plentiful rainfall on Madeira.

Jardim takes an original and somewhat experimental approach to the philosophy and practice of Madeira winemaking. He believes that the wine's longevity is due to partial, not full, oxidation during wine production. He has restored the company's ancient, giant wine vats, some of which are made from Brazilian satinwood and other non-oak woods. He believes in cleaning his smaller, American oak barrels every five years in order to clear out elements like bitartrate or flakes of heavy char from former bourbon barrels. In addition, he is sending barrels out of the winery, as well: seasoning barrels with young Madeiras for Scotch whisky and Irish whiskey producers. (The young Madeiras are in these new barrels for only a short time.)

As a winemaker, Jardim is open to experimentation in order to create more authentic, yet cleaner new wines. Henriques & Henriques continues to produce a full slate of all types of wines, and to bottle old stocks as necessary. The company has also acquired half a dozen Madeira brands over time, and they release wines under these brand names as well. Together, Henriques & Henriques and Justino's now produce more than 55 per cent of all Madeira wine by volume.

With an incredible stock of older vintages, Henriques & Henriques wines run the gamut of aromas and flavours from toffee to clear golden honey, from bright acidity to tropical fruit, from green grass to orange peel and preserved cherries. In its storehouse, Henriques & Henriques has solera wines dating back to an 1898 Sercial that is full of complexity. Other stand-outs include fifty- and sixty-year-old Boal and Terrantez and Sercial wines, all vividly alive, and younger, complex wines that seem barely ready for drinking even after two decades of ageing.

The company now known as Justino's was originally called Vinos Justino Henriques & Filhos when it was established in 1870. To avoid confusion with the Henriques & Henriques company, Justino's eventually dropped 'Henriques' from its name. The largest volume shipper of Madeira, Justino's has also subsumed more than half a dozen other Madeira companies over the years. In 1993 Justino's became part of a French spirits conglomerate, La Martiniquaise, and received an infusion of capital enabling the company to relocate a few years later from Funchal to an industrial park to the east of the city, higher up in the hills. There, Justino's have state-of-the-art production and ageing facilities, and room for experimentation as well. With the change in altitude and micro-climate, the Madeira ageing process has also altered in some ways, challenging the wine-makers to adapt to their new, cooler locations where the wines are expected to evolve more slowly than those made in earlier centuries, at a lower altitude.

Justino's also produces the local Colombo label Madeiras and table wines, as well as wines for the notable u.s.-based importer/

distributor Broadbent Selections. That company is run by the know-
ledgeable Bartholomew Broadbent, who also has interests in port
and other Portuguese and international wines. Justino's produces a
variety of Madeiras for Broadbent, including classic styles as well
as proprietary blends of limited availability. Broadbent is one of the
major promoters of Madeira in the United States.

There are 1,300 growers who supply grapes for Justino's, with
strict requirements for health and other aspects of the grapes' condition at harvest. Justino's wine-production area looks similar to
any modern winery, with a defined crushpad and steel fermentation
tanks – though they also have tanks with heatable jackets for the
estufagem process. They take care to avoid any oxidation until after
the wines are fortified. Justino's winemakers are enjoying tweaking
the flavours and aromas of their wines in a variety of barrels (used,
of course) from diverse wines and spirits including Sauternes,
Pineau des Charentes, Moscatel de Setúbal, Irish whiskey, Cognac
and Armagnac. They are also supplying some whisky barrels for
'Madeira-finished' Scotch.

In addition to their current releases of five-, ten- and fifteen-year-
old wines, they have stocks going back a hundred years (or perhaps
longer) in many styles. Their current colheita release is nearly twenty
years old. In bottles, they have a range of wines such as a youth-
ful and spicy fifty-year-old Terrantez, a sweet and spice-cake 1933
Malvasia and a tropical-fruit Boal from 1934.

Justino's holds a unique position among Madeira exporters: as
of 2002 it is the sole company allowed to export Madeira in barrels.
It does so once a year. The occasion is a multi-day Madeira Festival
held each year in early August, in the Massachusetts coastal city of
New Bedford. This city has long been home to many immigrants
from Portugal, from the Azores and now from Brazil as well, where
Madeira is well known as a fine wine.

One sole U.S. importer, Saraiva Enterprises, has received
authorization from IVBAM to import barrels of Madeira wine, and
this authorization must be renewed annually. After authorization,

Joe Saraiva has quantities of new 225-litre oak barrels delivered to Justino's in Madeira, where the barrels are tested and seasoned before being filled and shipped to the u.s. The barrels are opened with great excitement and fanfare at the beginning of the Feast of the Blessed Sacrament, an annual early August event that began in 1915; organizers believe this is the 'World's Largest Portuguese Feast'. Recently, the order has grown to thirty barrels, which is the equivalent of more than 9,000 bottles for each festival.

The Barbeito Company was founded right after the end of the Second World War, in 1946. Its motto is 'innovation and tradition'. The founder, Mário Barbeito, was an accountant who travelled abroad and thus familiarized himself with the best wines in Europe, so friends kept encouraging him to start his own business.

At that time, it was not uncommon to acquire barrels of Madeira for home consumption. Family members would have Madeira with cake for an afternoon snack; many people had a small glass every night before bed. It happened that his family had some stocks of old wines, barrels from as early as 1900, even one from 1863. And that is how the company began: by bottling the wines they owned, then sourcing more from friends, and eventually producing their own Madeira wines.

Barbeito also produces a set of specially blended Madeiras for the u.s.-based Rare Wine Company. Rare Wine developer Emanuel Berk (a u.s. importer and distributor) worked with current Barbeito winemaker Ricardo Barbeito, a grandson of the founder of the company, to create wines that reference historic blends, with names like Charleston Sercial, Savannah Verdelho, Boston Bual and New York Malmsey.

In 1991 the company was partially acquired by Kinoshita Shoji of Japan, and this enabled Barbeito to move to more spacious headquarters just outside Funchal, in Câmara de Lobos. There, they built a modern wine-production facility as well as a public tasting room, on a steep hillside overlooking the Atlantic Ocean. As mentioned earlier, Barbeito has become well known for its rare Bastardo Madeiras. This grape was popular before the phylloxera epidemic of the 1860s; very little of it was grown after that, but it has recently become highly prized to make modern Madeira wines so more vineyards are being planted. Because there has been such a small quantity of this grape available, Madeira winemakers there are still experimenting, still (re)learning about its characteristics.

Barbeito is committed to honouring the past as well as innovating where possible. While using a modern grape press for some grapes, they also have a small, round, robotic *lagar* (foot-treading basin for winemaking) to create more structured wines through this specific manner of crushing the grapes.

For ageing, they use old barrels from several countries including Hungary, France and Portugal, some of which formerly held red wine and others white wine, or so they believe. They note that in the past, it was less important to keep records of where the barrels came from, than to be assured that the barrels had been used – and used for wine – in order not to add other flavours or strong tannins and other wood-related characteristics to the wine.

Barrel of Madeira at the Henriques & Henriques wine company, with the seal of the POSEI programme that supports Madeira wine producers, encouraging traditional production methods and long ageing.

Experimentation, tradition and a combination of the two mark this very modern, popular company. Transparency is another of its hallmarks; the winemakers are open about providing barrel samples of their new, unblended wines to wine industry members, in order to educate them about the unique qualities of Madeira's grapes and wines.

Another small company still active today, J. Faria & Filhos, is a small business that was founded in 1949. They began to release modern Madeira wines only in 1993. The company is not well known outside of Madeira.

The newest and youngest Madeira producers are to be found at the CAF agricultural cooperative (Cooperativa Agricola do Funchal) under the name Madeira Vintners. This is an all-female wine production group – by happenstance, not by design. The Madeira Vintners winery itself is not a cooperative, but rather a special division of CAF. Madeira Vintners was established in 2012, and they were lucky enough to have a large and high-quality harvest of Tinta Negra grapes their first year. Their first winemaker, young Lisandra Gonçalves, is believed to be the first woman winemaker on the island. Madeira Vintners successfully released their debut wine, a three-year-old, in 2016, for CAF's 65th anniversary.

The company has found that a measure of feminine influence does enhance their wines. Their Madeiras are lighter both figuratively and literally because they do not add any caramel colouring, and they keep their alcohol down to the minimum 17 per cent. The wines have proprietary names, indicating levels of dryness and sweetness: Fenix is *seco* (dry), Poios is *meio seco* (medium dry), Citrine is *meio doce* (medium sweet) and Sobremesa is *doce* (sweet). In addition, they are working on some cocktail recipes, mainly made with their Poios Madeira. While continuing to work with Tinta Negra grapes, Madeira Vintners has also added a small amount of Complexa some years, and they also occasionally add some Listrão and Caracol grapes from Porto Santo.

Today and Tomorrow

These days Madeira producers are often defined by their entry-level wines. Partly this is because they are what most new wine drinkers first experience (the older wines being more expensive) and partly it is owing to the fact that capricious record-keeping and consolidation in the past means it can be difficult to establish the complete provenance of a wine, so producers want to be sure to display their individual flavour and aroma profiles to a new generation of consumers. In any case, there is still a lot to be discovered about Madeira wines, both current and historic.

Learning about Madeira these days can be an attempt to nail down a moving target. There are several reasons for this. One is that, as more analysis is done on vineyards, grapes, winemaking and ageing, improved knowledge spurs improvements in viticulture, winemaking and the wines themselves. In this way, time is on our side. But time is also the enemy, because as the years pass, more is forgotten about the great traditions of Madeira, about its grape sources, its winemaking processes and ageing, and about the personalities and the companies that created this legendary wine.

Further complicating the saga of Madeira is the lens of history: interpretations of the past change over time. So it's not only that memories are lost, it's that traditions are seen with new perspectives. This seems to be going on all over the landscape of Madeira, both on the island itself and in the countries that consume Madeira wine. For example, in some regions, Madeira is considered hopelessly old-fashioned. Yet in others, there's a new interest in Madeiras, so producers have responded by creating new, fresher and subtler wines. Still others discover Madeira because of a commitment to honouring a cultural heritage of food and wine. The growing tourism industry is yet another means for Madeira producers to generate interest in their wines, with tours and tasting rooms and sales to visitors.

High-end collectors and people in the wine industry are seeking out exceptional wines for themselves and their customers. They are fascinated with the wine's almost unbelievable ageability. In the wine world newly bottled Madeiras that are decades old are still considered new releases so they are periodically submitted to international wine competitions. Many win awards, thus inspiring renewed attention for Madeira on the world market.

5
Marsala

———

There are clear signals of a tiny renaissance on the western edge of the Italian island of Sicily. It involves the most famous historic wine of this region: Marsala. This legendary Italian wine was actually conceived and produced by British merchants in Sicily. It took the world by storm in the late eighteenth century, and remained a celebrated wine for over a century. Then it began a slow decline – until quite recently.

Currently, Marsala's older drinking traditions coexist with a somewhat modernized, upgraded version of the wine, thanks to a few excellent new wine producers and the odd restaurateur. For the connoisseur, there are some incredible collections of old Marsala wines being released now. These wines are rare and wonderful. So few people are aware of historic Marsalas that they may be somewhat difficult to find, but they are amazingly good value today.

The ancient port city of Marsala lies on the far northwestern tip of the roughly triangular island of Sicily, which is located in the Mediterranean Sea, just off the 'toe of the boot' of Italy's mainland. For several millennia, the island of Sicily has been a crossroads for travellers in the Mediterranean. The port of Marsala was historically one of the busiest on the island. It was here that Englishman John Woodhouse arrived in the early 1770s, planning to trade English cloth and clothing for raw goods from this part of Sicily. But when he tasted the strong wines made around Marsala, he realized they reminded him of the extremely popular Madeira wines from Portugal. Woodhouse determined to create a new Madeira-style wine, fortified for export, and sell it in Britain – which he did, quite successfully.

Current Marsalas ready for a wine-pairing dinner at the tiny Ciacco Putia Gourmet restaurant in the centre of the town of Marsala.

A few other Britons also saw the advantages of Marsala, and set up their own prosperous Marsala companies. So it happens that, essentially, Marsala wine as we know it was invented by the British in Sicily. It wasn't until the following century that the first Italians launched their own thriving endeavours in this flourishing industry. Florio is the most famous Marsala producer with an Italian (but not Sicilian) name. Still very well known today, Florio is also part of today's nascent renaissance of Marsala wine.

Fortified Marsala wines have some of the same aromatic and flavour elements that have appealed to so many wine drinkers over the centuries, especially people who have appreciated the fortified Madeira wines and the vins doux naturels of southern France. All of these wines have lively acidity and complex scents and flavours: nuts, dried fruits, salted caramel. Like vins doux naturels, Marsalas are produced in several tiers of ageing, and at a variety of levels of dryness and sweetness. And like Madeira in particular, the lion's share of Marsala is now used for culinary purposes, in the food industry and in home cooking – which has proved extremely unfortunate for its reputation as a fine wine.

Marsala wines are only a few percentage points higher in alcohol than table wines today, at around 18 per cent alcohol. Many of today's top-tier Marsala wines are embedded in the tradition of sweet wines of Sicily, and they are being rediscovered by wine-lovers and sommeliers who are looking for 'new' beverages to cap off a meal, either paired with small desserts or sipped on their own. Dry Marsalas are being paired with savoury foods, or sipped as aperitifs.

The town of Marsala.

Typical early spring view in Marsala: flowers flourish between the rows of dormant grapevines in a vineyard next to an olive orchard.

The Region of Marsala in the Crossroads of the Mediterranean

Marsala is the westernmost port on the island of Sicily, quite close to the coast of Africa; the distance between Sicily and Tunisia at that point is only 228 kilometres (142 mi.). For several millennia, Marsala has been a critical landing base for various peoples involved in trade, warfare and conquering territories in Europe and in Africa, as well as sequentially ruling the island of Sicily itself. For example, the Marsala area was an important settlement for the Phoenicians 3,000 years ago. Much later, in the third century BC, the Carthaginians retreated there during a long siege by the Romans in the Second Punic Wars; during that period the city of Marsala was known as Lilibaeum. Still later, mainly during the tenth century, the Muslims ruled this area. The name 'Marsala' is a contraction of the Arabic words for 'the port of Allah'. And even in the twenty-first century, quite a bit of Arabic influence remains in foods, names and other cultural elements in this part of Sicily.

By the early 1100s, the large Moorish (Arabic) realm was contracting, and the Normans conquered Sicily. Then the island was ruled by the Kingdom of Aragon, the Kingdom of Spain, briefly the Savoyards, the Austrians, then the Spanish Bourbons. The Kingdom of Two Sicilies (Naples plus Sicily) endured from 1815 until the campaign for the unification of Italy began under Giuseppe Garibaldi in 1860.

During all this time, while kings, nobles and powerful families jostled for money, power and ultimate rule, the regular inhabitants of Sicily seem to have gone along with their lives, receiving neither the spoils of war nor the benefits of peace. For many hundreds of years, ordinary Sicilians learned to keep their heads down and try to feed themselves with whatever little they had. Rulers were not in the habit of improving the lives of their subjects on this island. For centuries the peasants and small merchants here were forced to make do as they had since the Middle Ages, with outmoded methods in bare

subsistence farming and trading practices. This lasted well into the twentieth century.

One element that became ingrained in the culture was a deep conviction that one needed to take care of one's own. The 'help others' principles of Northern European religions did not penetrate to this southern Mediterranean island. In government and commerce, a tradition of 'protection' (which some called 'corruption') reigned, and families became their own small fiefdoms. Banditry was the effective rule of law. With no external support available, few Sicilians could muster enough education, experience or capital to invest in any types of improvements; they were not able to exploit their own island resources, either. This is where Marsala wine comes along.

When Europeans began travelling on their 'Grand Tours' of cultural history, though they considered Italy ragingly romantic, they rarely ventured out to the island of Sicily. The British and other Northern Europeans who made it to the island came as traders, looking for raw materials to export to their home countries. In 1770 John Woodhouse from Liverpool arrived in Marsala looking to establish a trading business. At that point in history there was a sense of alarm in Britain about a potential surplus of English wool and cloth that was generated by problems with the American market; justifiably so, because America would erupt into its Revolutionary War in 1775.

Woodhouse is reported to have been seeking to send materials such as almonds, coral, olive oil and sodium carbonate back to Britain, so it's likely he was open to whatever he could find. Sicily was already known as a source of agricultural goods such as almonds and olive oil for England and other Northern European countries. It was also becoming a significant source of mined sulphur, which is a critical element in many manufacturing processes. Some wines were also exported. These were mainly white wines, which often became

Just north of the city of Marsala, this shallow ocean bay still has its traditional windmill-driven saltworks.

slightly oxidized due to the normal vinification and transportation methods of the day.

Woodhouse found the island wines pleasant. Many of the vineyards abutted the coastline and this lent the wines a seaside freshness, balancing their sweetness in an attractive manner, especially for the tastes of the times. Some of the wines were made with grapes that had naturally high sugar contents and/or were harvested late in the season, and these turned into wines that were high in alcohol, which was another asset in trade. However, Marsala's climate remains warm through the autumn, and in many years, the wines had a tendency to begin to oxidize even before transit.

Woodhouse began testing the fortification of Marsala wines for their stability during transportation – and for more longevity in Britain. He was modelling his fortified Marsalas on the Madeira wines he was already familiar with. Because the costs of winemaking in Sicily were so low, Woodhouse planned to flood the market with his own less expensive version of Madeira. After some experimentation, he arrived at an effective formulation for his wines. This is how the wine we now know as 'Marsala' was created.

Apparently, Woodhouse had more trouble producing his wines in Sicily than he did selling them in Britain. Sicilian farmers did not have a mindset to produce their crops on order for someone else. They were accustomed to first feeding their families, then, in the rare event they had anything left, looking around to sell their surplus later. Also, in the western sections of Sicily, the only crop that farmers tended to grow with any surplus potential was grain. Grain will keep for weeks or months; it does not need to be harvested and used immediately, as do ripened grapes.

In order to acquire enough grapes to make his wines, Woodhouse offered to pay for the grapes in advance, and to lend money to farmers who needed it. He must have developed powerful incentives and enforcements because his whole system, which, though normal for a Northern European company, was entirely foreign to the Sicilian groups he was dealing with. However, Woodhouse ultimately succeeded. Perhaps the Sicilians were also influenced by Woodhouse's other activities, which included upgrading the infrastructure of Marsala. Woodhouse built jetties out into the sea to provide a safe harbour for merchant ships, and he paved (or cobbled) adjoining roads for ease of transportation of goods to the harbour. Owing to Woodhouse's background, the centre of Marsala, near the port, apparently resembles an eighteenth-century English city in its layout.

This bust of Giuseppe Whitaker, son of one of the Marsala industry's founders, Joseph Whitaker, welcomes visitors to the island of Mozia (also known as Motya). Giuseppe lived here and extensively excavated the island's Phoenician ruins in the early 20th century.

Reportedly, Woodhouse's payment systems also laid the ground-work for a modern system of banking in Sicily, which was lacking at that time.

As a combination winery and industrial estate, Woodhouse built himself a *baglio*: a large, high-walled space about the size of one square city block, enclosing his winery and storage for his wines. Even his own dwelling was part of the *baglio* because he felt he needed to be on site at all times. Woodhouse's *baglio* was built right on the coast, across the road from the sea, and some say the very tall walls were put in place to act as fortification against pirates. Romantic though this notion is (and there were pirates in the Mediterranean at that time), it is more likely that he was protecting his livelihood from banditry by the nearby inhabitants.

With the success of Woodhouse's foray into the wine industry, he needed help, so his brothers came over from England to work with him. He also got to know any important Britons who came to the area, one of whom was Lord Nelson, who arrived to 'escort' the Bourbon rulers to Palermo in 1798 after Napoleon had defeated them. At that time, Nelson also became an admirer of Woodhouse's Marsala, and he ordered large quantities to supply the fleet.

Lord Nelson was perhaps the first celebrity to endorse a wine. For his service to Sicily, he had been given an estate near Mount Etna that was known as the Bronte Estate, and he began to refer to himself as 'Bronte Nelson'. Not only did Lord Nelson allow Woodhouse to make public the fact that Woodhouse was supplying the Royal Navy, but he agreed to let Woodhouse call one of his Marsala wines 'Bronte Marsala'. This type of publicity didn't hurt, along with the fact that the flavours of the Marsala fortified wines hit a sweet spot in British taste. In a relatively short time, Marsala became extremely popular in England.

In 1806 the young Yorkshire merchant Benjamin Ingham came to Sicily to sell wool, and stayed to become a Marsala producer and exporter after he saw Woodhouse's operation. When Ingham began his business, Napoleon's continental blockade was in place, making it difficult for Britons to get wines from France, Portugal and even Madeira, so demand for Marsala escalated. Even after the blockade was broken, these newly popular Marsala wines were still sought-after. The British army, already deployed in the Mediterranean, continued to defend Sicily against Napoleon – and incidentally to protect British interests like the Marsala businesses.

A young, single gentleman (only 22 on his arrival in Sicily), Benjamin Ingham first had a business partner, but that didn't work out. In 1814 he wrote to his sister and asked her to send one of her sons to help out in the company – a not uncommon practice at the time. After this young man's unfortunate death in 1818, his sister sent another son to help Ingham in his growing production and trade. Various reports indicate that either two or three of his sister's sons came to Sicily, and/or two or three of his brother's sons.

However many nephews arrived, this would have definitely been something the Sicilians could understand: a business that comprised only family as partners. Joseph Whitaker was the nephew who worked most closely with his uncle, and he eventually took over the business. Both Ingham and Whitaker became immensely wealthy and influential members of Sicilian society as the business expanded into a diversified export and investment company. Ingham himself eventually married Sicilian royalty, and built several houses and villas in Palermo and western Sicily, some of which are still in existence today. By the time Ingham retired in 1851, the company included Marsala production, export of other Sicilian products such as soda ash and sulphur, and even investments in America – and it was worth the equivalent of billions in today's money.

The business continued to prosper under Joseph Whitaker. But Joseph's son, known as Giuseppe Whitaker (the last of the line), wasn't as enchanted by the Marsala business as his father had been. He apparently played the field, travelled and was interested in archaeology. His fascination played out on the island of Mozia (Motya), located in the bay just north of the town of Marsala. Mozia was believed to be the site of an ancient Phoenician settlement,

Marsala wines with a Whitaker label, in tribute to Joseph Whitaker, an early developer of the Marsala industry during the first half of the 19th century.

Workers on Whitaker Island train the grapevines in the ancient circlet shape most suitable for these dry, wind-blown vineyards. The Tasca d'Almerita winery has taken up the challenge of making a very good modern Grillo wine from these Tenuta Whitaker grapes.

and Giuseppe Whitaker found evidence and artefacts indicating that this island was in fact inhabited by the Phoenicians. They had constructed a port and a large town surrounded by vineyards and other agricultural lands. In those days, the island was connected to the mainland by a narrow land bridge ideal for defence.

Today, the land bridge is under water so day-tripping tourists take a ten-minute motor boat ride to visit the ruins and the excavations. Giuseppe Whitaker's residence has now been converted into a museum that houses the thousands of artefacts he and his crew dug up. Unfortunately, Giuseppe was not an accomplished archae-ologist and his dig was not carried out with scientific methods, so a certain amount of the chronology of history and later civilizations was lost in the excavation process. However, it has been possible to recreate a reasonably accurate impression of Mozia as inhabited by the Phoenicians, and a model exists in the museum.

During recent decades, the Giuseppe Whitaker Foundation, which currently maintains the island, has planted new olive groves and has contracted with one of the best wine producers in Sicily, Tasca d'Almerita, to oversee the vineyards. Tasca d'Almerita now produces a very good Grillo wine from the Grillo grapes growing on the island, on vines that are pruned in the ancient traditional, circular-arched shape, low to the ground.

Woodhouse, Ingham and Whitaker are the most famous and enduring British names in Marsala, but there were others – Joseph Hopps and Vincent Gill being two of them – though most of the information on these smaller producers has been lost to history.

With regard to non-Sicilian Marsala magnates, there is one incredibly influential family to mention: Florio. Florio is historically the most famous, and currently stands as emblematic of Marsala. The Florio family is not Sicilian in origin, which is still mentioned as significant today, two hundred years after their arrival on the island. The family came from Calabria, a mainland region that nearly adjoins Sicily to the northeast. The Florios were very entrepreneurial – unlike native Sicilians, it is implied. They were importers of quinine, which is made from the bark of the cinchona tree and had become very important in the 1700s as the only real treatment for malaria. (Cinchona is also an essential element in another fortified wine, vermouth, but it was not used in Marsala wine.)

The Florio Baglio, which has stood on the Marsala coast since shortly after the Florio winery was founded in 1832.

The Florios set up a pharmacy in Palermo to sell quinine, and they flourished. They sent their son Vincenzo to London and other European capitals, and when he inherited the family business he looked at various enterprise possibilities in Sicily and decided to become a Marsala producer in 1830. Unlike the British, the Florios did not have a ready export market at home, so they had to create their own customer base. At that time, there was no united country of Italy; there were various provinces in this geographical area, so the Florio company had free rein there to begin to promote and sell their 'Marsala Florio' brand wines.

As it happened, it was Marsala that helped Giuseppe Garibaldi (known as the unifier of Italy) conquer Sicily in 1860, and move his troops to the mainland: because of the improvements John Woodhouse had made in the port of Marsala, Garibaldi chose that as the location to land his vaunted army of a thousand 'red shirts', and proceed with his conquest. Either on his way back to his ships that time, or during a subsequent visit to Sicily in 1862, Garibaldi stopped at the Florio *baglio* and tasted the wines. Later Florio marketed a 'Garibaldi Marsala' because he had enjoyed this particular style of sweet wine. To this day there is an official category of Marsala called 'Garibaldi Dolce'.

Vincenzo Florio was as ambitious as Benjamin Ingham, and the two started a steamship company together, in order to export their wines more efficiently. Ingham also used his ships to bring back American oak to make wine barrels. Both Ingham and Florio sold their Marsala wines in the United States; Ingham personally travelled to Boston to open his market there.

Florio also built a large *baglio* by the sea, on the same road as the Woodhouse and Ingham/Whitaker operations. Florio's Marsalas were considered very high quality for many decades, and so the company justifiably took its place at the top, in the history of Marsala wine, by the middle of the nineteenth century.

Owing to Marsala's growth and table wine exports from other areas, wine grapes were now proving to be one of the best agricultural crops in Sicily. Then – as they had been all over Europe – the vine-yards were attacked by oidium (powdery mildew) in the middle of the 1800s. However, it was discovered that this condition was treatable by the application of sulphur, which happens to be mined in Sicily. The vineyards recovered quickly and were flourishing a few years later, though once again, it was the wine producers and exporters that saw the profits, not the peasant farmers.

Then came the second vineyard plague: phylloxera. There is no cure for phylloxera, an insect that burrows into the vines and the roots. When it appeared in European vineyards, it took many years to figure out what the problem was, and to instigate a remedy. As with the other wines discussed in this book, the only remedy was to replant every single vineyard with American, phylloxera-resistant rootstock, and graft the wine grapes onto the roots. Phylloxera moved through Europe beginning in the 1860s, taking fifty years to spread through the wine-producing regions of the continent.

Some of the French vineyards were decimated early in this period, in major wine regions like Bordeaux. Suddenly Sicilian wines of all styles were in great demand, often by French winemakers who engineered the Sicilian wines to make them appear to be French. With a scarce population in western Sicily, the farmers there were finally able to show some gains for their work – that is, if the profits weren't seized by the new organized crime groups that sprang up in this area.

Various Sicilian families finally decided to join the Marsala production business in the latter half of the nineteenth century, not long after the unification of Italy. They include front-runners like Rallo, Spano, Mineo, Martinez and a partnership of D'Allo & Bordonaro; however, few of them are in existence today. By the end of the nineteenth century there were forty Marsala producers in the area. Unfortunately, at the same time the dreaded phylloxera epidemic hit Sicily's vineyards, and essentially destroyed them. By then the French had replanted their vineyards with phylloxera-resistant rootstock, so they were back in business and suddenly no longer needed Sicily's wines.

A Perfect Storm in Marsala

Sicily had, of course, replanted its vineyards – and quite quickly. But a perfect storm of events conspired to thwart the renovation of the Marsala industry, and thus began its slow descent into near-oblivion for a hundred years. (Glimmers of hope began to appear on Marsala's horizon only very recently.)

What was the reason for Marsala's lengthy decline? There was no one particular cause. First, when their vineyards were destroyed by phylloxera in the late 1800s, the Marsala producers did what the French had done before them: they sourced grapes from elsewhere, and manipulated them into an approximation of the well-known Marsala wines. But they cut corners, and this is what first began to hurt them: the questionable quality of their wines.

Still, Marsala remained popular for some time in Northern European countries, and in the United States – locations that did not have their own domestic wine regions at the time, and were obliged to import all their wines. The number of Marsala producers still increased for a while, with so many Johnny-come-latelies in the field that there was no way quality wines could be the end result, both from lack of worthy materials and processes, and from lack of oversight in the industry. The net effect was (justifiable) distrust of the quality of Marsala wine, and a major downturn in the entire industry.

A second cause of Marsala's decline was an increase in worldwide wine production and a change in consumer taste that occurred at the beginning of the twentieth century. Wine traders began looking to import more table wines than speciality fortified wines in many areas of the world. Winemakers from France and Germany – and later from the mainland of Italy – began to export their table wines to consumers all over the globe who were acquiring a taste for them. Local production of spirits

Ironically, Marsala wines with additives, like this 'Cremovo', led to the popularity of 'adulterated' Marsala – which in turn accelerated a collapse of the category of fine Marsala wines in the mid-20th century.

Risotto made with Marsala wine is a well-known and popular dish throughout Italy.

such as brandy and rum also became competition for Marsala wines, especially in the New World, where populations were increasing.

Third, in Sicily, the population was decreasing. During the first decade or so of the 1900s, nearly a third of the inhabitants emigrated, most to New World countries, to take advantage of new opportunities there. Some Sicilians took their taste for Marsala with them, but because they were generally poor immigrants, the Marsalas exported to these countries tended to be very low-end wines.

World politics dealt a fourth and (nearly) fatal blow to the Marsala industry. Antagonism between Italy and the Austro-Hungarian Empire had resulted in closed borders for Italian products in 1904. Germany continued to be a lucrative market for Marsala and other Italian wines – until the outbreak of the First World War in 1914. And at the end of the war in 1918, everything was different, from society to commerce to politics. The beginning of the Prohibition era in the United States spelled the death of the u.s. Marsala trade in 1919. Even though there was some bootlegging during Prohibition, it mainly involved high-alcohol spirits, not wines, or even fortified wines in any quantities.

By then, Marsala producers were desperate. They went about trying to rebuild the industry in two different ways. One method was to create new 'versions' of Marsala that they thought would appeal to broader markets. They made Marsala into a dessert drink, a sweet zabaglione-flavoured beverage somewhat like eggnog, which people enjoyed – but mainly on holidays. The producers used additives such as eggs, almonds, cinnamon, vanilla, caramel and chocolate to create these Marsala products. They were especially popular in Italy, where, for much of the twentieth century, many people believed these bottled, sweet beverages were the real and true Marsala wines. In fact until the 1980s they were labelled as 'Marsala wine', though now they are not allowed to be labelled as such; they are termed 'liqueurs' and/or bear proprietary names, Cremovo being one of the most famous in Italy.

Producers also tried to rebuild their industry by promoting the use of Marsala wine in manufactured sweets, and in sweet and savoury sauces. This became very popular. But in the end it backfired because consumers began to see Marsala only as a culinary additive. In fact in the U.S. today, most people think of Marsala not as a wine, but as an undefined cooking ingredient solely for use in recipes such as veal Marsala and chicken Marsala.

Instead of rebuilding Marsala's reputation, these strategies for improvement effectively made Marsala, as a quality wine, disappear from the world stage. Consumer taste also moved towards fresher, fruitier and less oxidized wines. By the mid-twentieth century, it was apparent that the Marsala wine producers' dilution of the 'brand' of Marsala had caused its demise – almost.

How to Find, Serve and Drink Fine Marsalas

Marsala had been a fine wine for over a hundred years before its reputation stumbled. Consumers had savoured both the drier and sweeter versions of this elegant fortified wine, made in a variety of styles to appeal to the palates of different countries.

Today, it's important to serve Marsala slightly chilled, following the tradition in which it was made. A hundred or more years ago, homes were usually much cooler, and Marsala wine was made to be sipped at a temperature that is lower than our current room temperature; Marsala is best at around 12–18°C (around 55–65°F). The wine is served in smaller portions than table wines, a serving being around 100 ml (3 oz.). This encourages the drinker to sip it slowly, savouring the complex aromas and flavours and the long finish.

One of Marsala's best qualities is that it stores well for decades, unopened. A reliable wine purveyor can supply very old Marsalas that are wonderful to drink today. Once opened, a bottle of Marsala will keep well for weeks, even months. It's important to recork it and store it in a refrigerator or other cool, dark place. This makes it easy for a consumer today to acquire and sample a range of Marsalas, and to understand and appreciate their finer aspects.

When first experiencing Marsala, it's best to start with Marsala Vergine, which is considered the purest (or most 'virgin') Marsala. It offers an authentic array of aromas and flavours, from nuttiness to saltiness, with some strains of dried fruit. Next, on the list would be gold-coloured (*oro*) *Marsala Superiore* and *Superiore Reserva*, made in both dry (secco) and off-dry (semisecco) styles. Marsala wines have a substantial amount of acidity, so even the somewhat sweeter wines will be well balanced.

Ambra (amber) Marsalas in dry and sweet styles will provide an interesting contrast of colour and flavour, as will the relatively rare *Rubino* (ruby), which is made with red grapes, not white grapes like all the other Marsalas.

When tasting, it's best to begin with the secco styles and move on to semisecco and then dolce (sweet). The secco and semisecco styles work best as aperitifs and can also be sipped during the meal. These are rich wines that may be served with light dishes such as arancini filled with fish, cheese or vegetables, some of the many Sicilian versions of caponata, and various light pasta dishes with vegetables or seafood (but not with non-Sicilian sauces such as

Marinara or Bolognese). Semisecco Marsalas also pair well with a variety of Italian cheeses, ranging from slivers of pithy Parmigiano Reggiano to dollops of pungent Gorgonzola.

The Marsala dolces are stunning with dessert dishes of all types, from fruit to cream to chocolate. In the city of Marsala one of the most traditional pairings for the semi-sweet wines are the almond-studded biscotti called *tagliancozzi*. With the sweeter Marsalas, the extra-rich Sicilian cassata cream cake is a perfect match.

The Evolution of Marsala Production

The wines made in Marsala start out naturally high in alcohol because the ripened grapes' sugar content is high. Yeast converts grape sugar to alcohol, so high-sugar grapes = high-alcohol wine. This means that relatively less neutral spirit is needed to fortify the wines to proper levels, a cost measure which could have been another reason for John Woodhouse's choice of the Marsala location for his wine business.

Most likely, the wine that Woodhouse first tasted was *vino perpetuo*, a naturally high-alcohol wine that was oxidized, made in solera. The solera is a system (most common in sherry production) whereby wine in casks is aged until some of it is taken out when it is ready to be bottled. At that time, a younger version of the same wine is added to the original casks in order to fill them up to the desired level. Because barrels are never emptied, the wine inside is essentially *perpetuo* (perpetual). The barrels are not completely filled with wine, which gives the wine the opportunity to interact with oxygen (to become oxidized) and is another factor in the longevity of the finished wine.

Marsala was one of the first wines in Italy to receive the country's official DOC (*Denominazione di Origine Controllata* or Controlled Denomination of Origin) status a few years after this national system was established in the 1960s; Marsala DOC was created in 1969. However, this occurred during a period when many Marsala wines were made and sold cheaply, with various additives allowed. While increasing the market for Marsala sales for culinary uses, the overall effect of these liberal regulations was to severely compromise Marsala's reputation. When global wine consciousness broadened in the 1980s, consumer awareness of wine quality also increased. So the Marsala wine DOC regulations underwent a major rewrite in 1984 to tighten regulations on all aspects of Marsala wine production, from vineyard requirements and vinification techniques to wine categories and labelling. It is interesting to note that because of Marsala's relationship to British producers and the British market, Marsala wine labelling is officially allowed to appear in either Italian or English.

Grapes

Before John Woodhouse put together his famous fortified Marsala, the *vino perpetuo* and other wines he sampled were usually made with three main grapes, as is Marsala today. These grapes are Catarratto, Grillo and Inzolia (also known as Insolia or Ansonico) – though at different times, one or another grape dominated, due to climactic conditions. Currently Marsala is generally spoken of as being made mainly with Grillo, though it is possible that this is simply the most recognizable Sicilian white grape today, which is why it is most often cited. A fourth grape, Damaschino, is also currently allowed, but it is considered a lesser grape in terms of contributing to the typicity of Marsala wines. All of these are white grapes.

There is a small percentage of red Marsala made. It is called *rubino* now; formerly it was known as 'ruby' but a decision was made in the European community that the English word 'ruby' was so closely allied to descriptions of port (from Portugal) that Italy's Marsala region lost this naming right. In Marsala Rubino the following grapes may be used: Perricone (also known as Pignatello), Nero d'Avola (also known as Calabrese), Nerello Mascalese, and/or up to 30 per cent of the four white grapes listed above.

As in the rest of Italy, the DOC wine regulations require specific conditions. Marsala wine vineyards and wineries must be located in a designated area around the city of Marsala. The grapes must be grown in dry, elevated calcareous or clay soils, with plenty of sun, near or facing the Mediterranean Sea. The type of spirit added to Marsala for fortification is also specified to be grape-based, from the same grapes used to make the wine. Everything from the allowable methods of vine-growing to grape yields and harvesting is also regulated. In addition, the traditions of the wines and of the people of this land are honoured in these DOC rules.

Ageing Golden Wines: The Types of Marsala

There are several different categories of Marsala wine, based on dryness, sweetness, method of production and age. Marsala is categorized mainly by colour and age, with production and ageing methods specified for each style of the wine, as mentioned previously.

The largest percentage of Marsala is *oro* (gold); there is also a substantial amount of *ambra* (amber), and a very small amount of *rubino* (ruby). Needless to say, these names reflect the actual colours of the wines.

After the vinification process is complete, including fortification, ageing requirements for the different categories are one year for Marsala Fine, two years for Superiore, four years for Superiore Reserva, five years for Vergine and ten years for Vergine Reserva. Vergine Reserva can also be called Stravecchio (extra old). These requirements are minimums for each category and the actual ageing can be longer.

Another factor is that grape must (unfermented or partially fermented grape juice) is allowed to be added to the wine after vinification, both for colour and for sweetening. This additive is only permitted in Marsala Fine, Marsala Superiore and Superiore Reserva, and it is added to the finished wine before any ageing occurs. There are very strict rules about the fact that the must is required to come from the same grapes that the wine is made with. The process and/or formulation for adding grape must to the wine is called *concia*.

One type of additive is a cooked or boiled must, *mosto cotto*, which also adds sweetness to the wine. *Mosto cotto* is a darker colour than fresh or fortified must so when added to the wine, it can make the wine appear older. Some say it makes the Marsala look a more authentic colour. However, in the past, there was a huge problem with additives that were intended to disguise the actual age of the wine, or to create a counterfeit Marsala out of other wines. Today, higher-quality wines do not contain *mosto cotto*. However, *mosto cotto* may have been used in legitimate Marsalas in the past when Marsalas were deliberately customized for particular countries where the consumers had specific expectations for the colour as well as the flavour of their Marsala wines.

The modern winemakers who are responsible for the current small renaissance in Marsala are insulted by even a question about *mosto cotto* because they want their wines to be as fresh and authentic as possible. Instead, for both sweetness and alcohol adjustment in the vinified wines, they use *sifone*, which is made from fresh juice or must (*mistella*) that comes from the same grapes they used to make their Marsala wine. The must may be concentrated by evaporation or other natural methods, but not by cooking. Any fermentation of this juice is stopped at a specified point by fortification, using a spirit that is made from the same as the grapes used for Marsala wine.

Vergine and Vergine Reserve (aka Vergine Stravecchio) are dry Marsalas. All the other types can be made in all three categories of sweetness: secco (dry), with up to 40 grams/litre of residual sugar; semisecco (off-dry, also sometimes called semi-sweet) with 40–100 grams/litre; and dolce (sweet) with over 100 grams/litre. In the final product Marsala Fine is required to have a minimum of 17.5 per cent alcohol, while the other categories must have at least 18 per cent.

By far the largest amount of Marsala produced (around 80 per cent or more) is Marsala Fine, which is also the category specified for culinary manufacturing. Most Marsala Fine is used in the production of all types of food products from sauces to sweets to other drinks. This is the only category of Marsala that does not need to undergo a full ageing process if it is sold in bulk as a culinary additive, and not bottled for wine consumption. The companies that produce bulk Marsala Fine must declare its purpose at the start of their production period; this is also monitored by the Ministry of Agriculture, and the finished product must comply with all regulations of the countries it is exported to.

There is also plenty of drinking-quality Marsala Fine (also used by home cooks) sold in bottles in wine shops and supermarket wine departments. This Marsala Fine must be aged in wood – usually oak but cherry is also allowed – as is the case for the higher categories of Marsala. The size of the barrels or vats for ageing is not specified, and much of the older Marsala is kept in very large wooden containers, up to 1,000 or 2,000 litres (as opposed to traditional French wine barrels of just over 200 litres in Bordeaux and Burgundy). The large vat size drastically minimizes the wine's contact with wood, so the large vats are referred to as 'neutral' wood. These containers are proudly used for decades by the winemakers, and are kept in good repair with wooden pieces replaced as needed over time.

Labelling is also specified in the DOC regulations. In addition to the categories and styles of Marsala mentioned above and their specific rules, the word *Vecchio* (old) can be used on labels of Marsala that is Superiore category or older. Styles of wine can also be indicated on the labels with the traditional words and abbreviations that were created to market Marsalas in the past. Marsala Fine wine labels can also contain the term IP or *Italia Particolare*. (The word 'particular' or *particulare* means 'special' here.) Sometimes the country or the city inspired the name of a style of Marsala. For example, IP or *Italia Particolare* (Italian Particular) reflects the consumer taste of this country. LP (London Particular) and SOM (Superior Old Marsala) are terms used in English on Marsala labels, reflecting the long British history with this wine. Currently, these names can be used only in specific categories of Marsala. Marsala Superiore wines can also be labelled as LP or London Particular or *Inghilterra* (England); SOM or Superior Old Marsala; or GD or *Garibaldi Dolce* (Garibaldi Sweet).

More Marsala, Less Marsala in the Twentieth Century

A great deal of consolidation transpired in the fading Marsala industry during the twentieth century. Several of the larger and older Marsala producers had united under the famed Florio name in the early 1900s. Then the whole Florio company was acquired by the great Italian aperitif producer Cinzano, which was headquartered in northern Italy, in 1924. Five years later, Florio/Cinzano also assimilated what was left of the once-great Woodhouse and Ingham/Whitaker Marsala production companies, under the Florio name.

However, owing to a number of factors – including world wars, alterations in commerce and politics, and the evolution of consumer taste – by the middle of the twentieth century all that was left in the field were basically a few large, industrial Marsala companies, along with a smattering of very small producers. Almost all of the Marsala production then was for culinary purposes; there were also flavoured wines in Italy, and some (variable-quality) drinking wines that were trading on the vanishing reputation of this incredibly popular and distinguished wine of the eighteenth and nineteenth centuries.

Millennial Revival

From a high of around a hundred Marsala companies in 1950, there are approximately 25 today, and most are not large producers. It wasn't until the 1980s that the few Marsala producers who were left really woke up to the imminent danger of the extinction of this once-great wine, and a small flurry of activity has ensued. Producers of new wines stepped up their game in terms of quality. Old stocks of Marsalas were uncovered and offered for sale. And several wineries enthusiastically initiated oeno-tourism venues, constructing new wine boutiques, actively promoting their tours and tastings to tourists and to the general public. Only a couple of major producers remained from the 1800s; Florio and Pellegrino are the best known today.

The Pellegrino company (not the bottled water group) is currently also a significant factor in the popularity and availability of Marsala wines in Sicily and abroad. The official name of the company is Carlo Pellegrino. This wine production company was founded in 1880 by Paolo Pellegrino, a Sicilian notary who wanted to make wine. Ten years later, the company opened their Marsala production company and cellars. Their exports dramatically increased during the twentieth century, and the company diversified into table wines too.

In 2014 the Pellegrino company constructed a new, glass-enclosed oeno-tourism centre, Ouverture, in the city of Marsala. Pellegrino's wine tours contribute to tourism in the area, as well as to an increase in worldwide Marsala awareness. Pellegrino Marsalas are now available in other parts of Italy, in the U.S. and UK, and in other countries including France, Germany and Russia.

The venerable and historic Florio company is also a major part of the renaissance of interest in Marsala wines, both with its distinguished wines, its tasting room and lively boutique, and its nearly two centuries of authentic history. In 1998 this august Marsala company was acquired from Cinzano by another Italian beverage conglomerate, Illva Saronno, the parent company of the producer of the famed Amoretto di Saronno. Florio is now a significant player in the tourism business in Marsala, as well as continuing to produce excellent Marsala wines.

Of the currently active Marsala wine companies, a significant proportion of them are not producers. Instead, they mainly sell old stocks of great Marsalas they have stored, or have acquired – quality wines that were produced many decades ago and held by the families that produced them, or perhaps family friends that bought the wines for their own use. There are only three large companies and about ten small ones actively producing Marsala now. Among the smaller companies are Alagna, Buffa, Curatolo Arini, Francisco Intorcia, Lombardo, Martinez, Mirabella, Pipitone Spano and Rallo.

Rallo is an old name but its current incarnation is new. The well-established firm Diego Rallo & Figli had been a family-owned Marsala company for over a hundred years. Rights to the Rallo name were acquired in 1997 by the Vescos, a family that produced wine and olive oil, and now also makes several Marsalas that are available in Italy and Europe. (The Rallo heir and his wife had decided to establish a new table wine company with world-class wines, which turned out to be one of the best and most well-known modern wineries in Sicily: Donnafugata.)

Several of the other smaller Marsala companies have extremely good wines. Cantine Mirabella is one of them – though this company is based on old stocks of wine, which are limited. Pipitone Spano is very good as well. Francisco Intorcia's wines are considered excellent. Additional companies' wines are mainly found in the Marsala area, but one never knows: it's possible that some of these modern, classic and/or traditional Marsalas may turn up on the shelves of any wine shop, in any country, depending on the vagaries of import and interest.

In the late twentieth century one man in particular was instrumental in sparking the early stages of the beginnings of the revival of Marsala wine – a nearly infinitesimal movement that is still growing very, very slowly. This was Marco de Bartoli. De Bartoli came from one of the old Marsala families, and he was determined not to let the greatness of Marsala wines fade into nothingness – which is the direction it was headed.

De Bartoli began producing his own Marsalas and acquiring old stocks of great Marsala wines for bottling and blending. In addition, he made his own *vino perpetuo*-style wine which he called Vecchio Samperi (also the name of his family winery). It is a high-alcohol but unfortified dry wine, oxidized, nutty, with plenty of acidity. It is made in the solera system, becoming slightly sweeter with age through evaporation. De Bartoli believed that Vecchio Samperi was critical

At the Marco de Bartoli winery, traditional as well as modern winemaking techniques are used, including the large amphorae pictured here.

to the understanding of the development of Marsala – in addition to being a fascinating wine to drink. He wanted this unfortified wine to be included in the realm of Marsala DOC wines as a critical component of Marsala wine history: it is the original style of wine that John Woodhouse would have sampled when he arrived in Marsala in the 1770s. However, Vecchio Samperi is an unfortified wine, and so was excluded.

De Bartoli's crusade caused an uproar in the Sicilian wine community in the 1990s and early 2000s, just as the major producers of table wines were upgrading their vineyards and vinification, ready to take on the world in terms of quality. It took some years before all sides were reconciled; now De Bartoli's wines are esteemed in Sicily, as they are throughout Italy and in many other countries.

An important example of the 'new style' of Marsalas is the Marco De Bartoli winery's Vigna La Miccia, made exclusively with Grillo grapes and aged for five years. It is a semisecco wine, chilled during the vinification. This is common with modern white table wines, but was revolutionary in Marsala production. A contemporary style is also revealed in the final step of the making of this wine: it is not oxidized during ageing. This resulting wine is fresh and grapey, while also having classic, nutty notes, with hints of dried fruits.

Today, De Bartoli is recognized and respected as a crusader in Marsala and a valued winemaker, though his path was far from smooth. Unfortunately, Marco De Bartoli died in 2011, at the relatively young age of 66. The Marco De Bartoli winery, now run by his son and daughter, is currently one of the most respected in this part of Sicily.

At the Marco De Bartoli winery, there is a small shop where their wines can be purchased. And this is the trend in other wineries in the area: tasting rooms and shops at the wineries that welcome global tourists as well as day-trippers from Marsala. There are Marsala tours through the city and countryside, where historic *bagli* used for wine- and olive oil-production can be seen on the hills, many in ruins but some restored for winemaking or as residences or hotels.

In the city of Marsala today, aside from the massive Florio enterprise, little remains of the once-great Marsala wineries, or of the founding winemaker names

Marco de Bartoli, a leader in the revival of Marsala, also makes some of its wine with the solera (sherry-style) method of ageing.

of Woodhouse, Ingham and Whitaker. The Ingham *baglio* is in this same section of road; it was deserted as of this writing, but it appeared that an attempt at renovation had begun at some time in the not-too-distant past.

Woodhouse's *baglio* is still in existence in Marsala, with a new life. It now houses a lovely restaurant and other businesses. The restaurant, I Bucanieri, serves excellent beef because it is owned by a third-generation butchering family. Aware of their historical location, the restaurant owners also make a splendid Sicilian cassata to accompany their sweet Marsala wine selections.

Along the same stretch of road one can still find the bustling Florio *baglio* dating from 1830 – but now encompassing a super-modern wine shop and tasting room, with historic barrels of Marsala proudly displayed.

6

Vin Doux Naturel

—◆—

The noble fortified wines of Roussillon are a superb blend of sweet and savoury, history and modernity. They come from a little-known part of France where this type of wine was invented more than seven hundred years ago. This style of wine, called vin doux naturel, is exquisitely long-ageing, with colours extending from golden-brown to pale garnet and deep purple. Flavours range from cherries, berries and honey to seaside minerality, from tropical fruit and citrus to baking spices, along with notes of caramel, coffee and nuts.

Vin doux naturel originated along the southern edge of France at the Spanish border, in what is now the French province of Roussillon. (Vin doux naturel is pronounced *van doo nah-tue-RELL* and it is often abbreviated as VDN.) Translated literally, vin doux naturel means 'natural sweet wine'. This can be confusing when taking into account that VDNs are not table wines, but fortified wines. In the case of vin doux naturel, the term 'naturel' (natural) refers to the fact that the wine is 'naturally' sweet, and no sugar or other sweetener has been added to the finished wine. Instead, the natural grape sweetness remains when the fermentation process has been interrupted by fortification. This means that at a certain point in the winemaking process, distilled spirit is added to the wine in order to arrest the

The wild, dry, hilly countryside of Roussillon where grapes for vins doux naturels are grown.

fermentation. In addition, the liquid used to fortify the wine is also a 'natural' spirit, distilled only from grape products; it is essentially a clear, un-aged grape-based brandy.

Despite its centuries of magnificent, fortified wine-making, Roussillon is now struggling, and in two areas. First, Roussillon is faced with the problem that very few people today even know about their wonderful VDN wines. (However there is some basis for optimism here because VDNs have lately become a type of micro-cult wine favoured by wine directors who have discovered the wines' brilliant flavours and tones; these sommeliers are featuring them on restaurant wine lists in small amounts, generally as dessert wines.)

Second, in the late twentieth century, Roussillon was made part of the larger Languedoc-Roussillon wine region, and was over-shadowed by the Languedoc's wine reputation, which, at that time, was known for cheap and cheerful holidays along with exuberant, low-priced wines. Neither the Languedoc wines (many of which have since improved) nor its geographic location are representative of the adjacent, secluded area of Roussillon.

Culturally, Roussillon is Catalan, through many centuries of heritage. The inhabitants of Roussillon think of their province as 'North Catalonia', which is, in fact, Roussillon's genetic identity. It shares a long history with the Spanish Catalan region; only for the past few hundred years has Catalonia been divided by the political border between France and Spain. However, it is important to note that the Roussillon Catalonians are not part of the current Spanish separatist movement.

(Confusingly, there is also a small town named Roussillon in the Vaucluse department of France, some 400 kilometres (245 mi.) northeast of this wine region of Roussillon. That little Vaucluse town is unrelated to the discussion of this Roussillon and its VDN wines.)

Roussillon: Epicentre of Fortification

For more than seven centuries, Roussillon has staked its name and reputation on its sweet wines. As early as the thirteenth, fourteenth and fifteenth centuries, Roussillon's elegant Muscat wines were served at the tables of the regional nobility and rulers, even Pope Benoît III in his Avignon palace. At that time, the quality of Roussillon's red Grenache wines was appreciated as far away as Flanders.

Roussillon is considered the heart of VDN country. While there are currently small amounts of vins doux naturels made in a few other areas of southern France, these are small, individual regions which will be discussed later. Roussillon has had a reputation for growing quality grapes since the medieval period. With a prevalence of rocky hillsides in the region, the farmers sensibly put their grapes on the slopes, saving what little flatlands there were for grain to feed the populace.

VDNs are unique in that not only are they fortified wines, but they are often deliberately oxidized, and subjected to heat, cold and direct sunlight, during their production. It's not unusual to drive by wineries of all sizes and see large, clear glass, wine-filled jars proudly arranged in rows outside in order to age properly. They weather the elements through the chill rains of winter and the baking rays of the Mediterranean's long summer. When ready to drink, the bottled wines have an incredible capacity to meld savouriness with sweetness, blossoming from floral aromas to dried fruits, yet finishing in a pure balance on the palate. And the wines retain their excellence for decades upon decades.

A Corner of History

Several geographical factors have contributed to Roussillon's isolation. It is an area without major trade routes and thus with a noticeable lack of cultural dilution. For these reasons, when exploring the vin doux naturel wines of Roussillon, its origins and history can be perceived quite easily.

Although it was first part of the Kingdom of Majorca, then the Kingdom of Aragon, Roussillon has remained remarkably undisturbed since the Middle Ages, in its quiet corner of what is now France. The region is bordered by a crescent of coastline along the Mediterranean Sea, encircled by the Pyrenees to the southwest. The lower Corbières range, which comprises the eastern foothills of the Pyrenees, delineates the northern border of Roussillon.

All of France's vins doux naturels are produced in the southern part of France, close to the location where the process of fortifying wine was first codified and used to great effect. Fortification spread through this part of Europe after being introduced by Arnaud de Villaneuve (or Vilanova), the thirteenth-century scholar and physician from the Kingdom of Aragon who is widely believed to be the originator of the concept of fortifying wine. He used the Arab-originate process of distilling grapes, which he then added to local wine to make it stronger, mainly for medicinal purposes. In Roussillon, the fortification of wine was raised to a high art in the course of a few centuries, and fortified products expanded to include fine drinks as well as medicaments. During the 1600s, Roussillon wines were esteemed by nobility and political figures in the region, and by customers as far away as the area now known as Belgium.

The wines of Roussillon continued to be exported during the seventeenth century despite that being a period of political turmoil. In the middle of the century, Louis xiv of France sought to enlarge the official borders of France and encapsulate his country geographically. He wanted the Pyrenees to be the southern border of France – no matter that the eastern Pyrenees mountains ran through the region of Catalonia, which was under the rule of the Kingdom of Aragon. But by the mid-1600s, the power of the Aragon kingdom was waning and Louis xiv was able to secure France's southern border with the Treaty of the Pyrenees in 1659.

The treaty bisected Catalonia, leaving one section in France and the other in what is now Spain. As rulers do, France's Louis xiv wanted to assimilate the northern Catalonians into France, in order to create and maintain cultural homogeneity in his large kingdom, as well as to consolidate his power. He annexed the two most northern provinces of Catalonia – all of Rosselló and part of Cerdanya – and he gave this region a French name: Roussillon.

Historically, these were not fertile agricultural lands and they had little to recommend them to Louis xiv other than their geographical location. In terms of industry, over the course of millennia there had been only a few small iron and gypsum mines and ironworks, and for a short time in the modern era, a small amount of local silk production. A few little port cities in the eastern section offered a modest amount of sea-trade potential. And there was always a bit of the usual coastal enterprise of smuggling. Otherwise most people survived on subsistence farming. Life for the inhabitants of Roussillon continued in the same manner for several centuries, basically from the Middle Ages until well into the twentieth century.

Over the years, there were numerous efforts by the French kings and later by elected officials to integrate the Catalonians into France

Collioure village on the Mediterranean Sea with its iconic castle.

Vins doux naturels vineyards protected by the surrounding mountains in the region of Roussillon, France.

and French culture. The leaders of France forced the Catalonians to comply with certain governmental regulations and justice systems. However, the French failed to integrate the Catalonians culturally in any meaningful way. Elements of Catalan culture and language endure to this day in many aspects of life in the region, from the foods of the region to the area's public signage, which is written in both French and in Catalan. As a poor region that was not capable of supporting a large population – and whose inhabitants are self-identified (non-French) Catalonians – Roussillon has effectively kept to itself for centuries.

In wine development, towards the end of the 1700s, the Grenache grape became widely grown throughout southern France and northern Spain. Roussillon was sandwiched in between two larger and more well-known areas, Languedoc in France and Tarragona in Spain, which were able to produce and market large quantities of their Grenache table wines. Roussillon was left to continue specializing in its famed sweet wines, which at the time were made in both fortified and unfortified versions. Some of Roussillon's wines remained unfortified because the alcohol for fortifying was taxed by the state, and small winemakers could not afford the taxed product. However, today all of Roussillon's VDN wines are fortified.

During the first half of the nineteenth century, railways were built throughout France, wine production increased in Roussillon and exports grew. But this happy circumstance lasted only for a short time before two successive European grapevine plagues hit the region. First came oidium (powdery mildew), in the middle of the century. Oidium turned out to be curable with the application of sulphur. However, in some cases the vines were pulled out and replaced with other crops before this was discovered; it took time for the growers to decide to replant vineyards. Not long after the growers learned how to control oidium, the completely devastating phylloxera grapevine infestation began to spread from south to north throughout Europe. It took decades to figure out the cause of this devastation and disseminate information on the remedy, so during the second half of the 1800s there were many years of deprivation for the vineyard farmers and their families as the infestation worsened, and their vines produced fewer and fewer grapes. Even after the rootstock remedy was effected, there were further years to wait after replanting (which itself was not inexpensive) until the vines were old enough to bear fruit. In Roussillon, the Catalan people suffered immensely during this time, the economic crises pushing them further and further into poverty. They made little enough on their grapes because they didn't have the capital or infrastructure to make wine commercially. This meant they sold their grapes to producers, who realized most of the profits.

In the early 1900s the (mainly Catalan) growers held wide-ranging demonstrations throughout the region; these caused disruption, but little or no progress was made financially. Finally, the growers bravely took things into their own hands: they established cooperatives for winemaking and for distilling (to create the grape-based brandy for fortification). The peasant revolts and the resulting cooperative movement did help ameliorate the dire poverty of the Catalan growers for many decades.

Aged vin doux naturel from the Maury designation, produced by La Coume du Roy.

Ironically, during the same period as the vine plagues and grower protests, there were several positive developments for Roussillon's vins doux naturels. A new ruling was passed in 1872 that recognized Roussillon as the origin of these celebrated sweet, fortified wines, and gave them their own official tax status – which slightly increased profitability for the winemakers. This was called the Arago law, named after the Roussillon businessman who championed it. In 1898 the Pams law defined the term 'Vin Doux Naturel'. And in 1914, the Brousse law codified the production of VDNs by listing authorized grapes and other necessary regulations for the wines. These rules formed a regional pathway that led towards a national movement: the institution of France's first countrywide wine regulations in the 1930s, called AOC (*Appellation d'Origine Contrôlée*, or Controlled Designation of Origin). Roussillon's Rivesaltes, Maury and Banyuls VDNs were among the first in France to be awarded AOC status.

(The designation 'Roussillon' continues to be used in regard to wines, and Roussillon's regional wine boundaries have remained unchanged for the past century. However, politically, France has recently reorganized some of the country's administrative areas

– and their names. The result is that the political region once known as Roussillon is now part of the newly created and newly named French section called 'Occitanie'. Occitanie is a large district that contains both the former Languedoc-Roussillon and Midi-Pyrénées sections of France.)

The Sun, the Wind and the Grapes

Roussillon is a very sunny region, with hot, dry summers, moderate winter temperatures and a tremendous amount of wind. But the gales in this climate keep the grapes healthy: gusting winds prevent diseases from taking hold in the vineyards. There is a fair amount of rain in Roussillon but it often falls in torrents, pelting down so hard that it runs off the hills and doesn't soak into the vineyards. The VDN vines are old vines with deep roots, able to withstand this type of stress and to continue to produce grapes that are quite aromatic and flavourful, with good structure and acidity.

Topographically, valleys stretch finger-like from the Mediterranean coast into the hills where the grapes are grown. Much of the land is stony, some with silt or sand. There are also several areas with different types of soil such as clay, limestone or schist. The boundaries of these different soil types define the sub-regions of the Roussillon vine-growing areas for different VDN delimited areas: AOP (formerly AOC) Rivesaltes, Muscat de Rivesaltes, Maury, Banyuls and Banyuls Grand Cru.

Ever since fortified wines were first produced here, the Muscat grape has featured prominently in the wines. Actually, there are two types of Muscat grown in Roussillon. The most widely grown is Muscat à Petits Grains (small-berried Muscat), which has been grown in this area for thousands of years and is popular in many Mediterranean countries. The Muscat of Alexandria grape was brought to Roussillon by the Romans. Roussillon is the only region to produce VDN wines with this grape. It is difficult to make a great, balanced sweet wine with Muscat of Alexandria, which requires a

Banyuls-sur-Mer and Collioure hillside vineyards in Roussillon, France.

Grapes for Banyuls wines are grown on traditional 'bush vines' on the dry hillsides overlooking the town of Banyuls-sur-Mer on the Mediterranean coast.

special terroir, and this grape is authorized for VDN production in AOP Muscat de Rivesaltes. It is also used in small quantities in the *ambré* version of AOP Muscat de Rivesaltes and in AOP Maury Doux Blanc and AOP Banyuls Blanc.

Grenache, as mentioned earlier, was popularized in the 1700s. Roussillon's VDNs can also be made with any of three Grenache variations: *noir* ('black' or red), *blanc* (white) and *gris* (grey). Until very recently, the different types of Grenache vines were interplanted, but now this system is being abandoned in favour of separate vineyards for each grape. It's a rather poignant decision considering that some of these strong, gnarled old vines have been growing side by side, white, red and grey, for up to a hundred years.

Additional grapes are authorized for different styles of vin doux naturel made in certain areas of Roussillon. These grapes include some older varieties – Carignan Noir, Macabeu and Tourbat (which is also known as Malvoisie du Roussillon) – and some more international grapes like Syrah. To complicate things further, VDNs are not only made in different styles, but in different colours as well, depending on the grapes and the method of production. Each AOP has strict descriptions for which types of wines can be produced there.

Wine Production and Styles

In basic terms, a VDN is made from a wine whose alcoholic fermentation is arrested by fortification: the addition of a small amount of neutral alcohol. Stringent regulations were put into place at the end of the nineteenth century to ensure the purity of the alcohol. Now, all the alcohol used for fortification must be 'of vinic origin'. This distillate is controlled by the French government in production and sale to the winemakers.

In French, the process of adding alcohol during VDN vinification is called *mutage*. Between 5 per cent and 10 per cent of the volume of the must (pressed grape juice) is added, and it is done at a precise time in the fermentation process. The finished wines must have an alcohol content of 15.5 per cent to 18.9 per cent.

Some wines are made with a slightly different process called *muté sur grains* or *muté sur marc*. This means that the unpressed grapes are macerated and fermented for a short time before the alcohol is added. The grapes are then further macerated with the alcohol for up to three weeks before the grapes are pressed. This is done for the enhancement of structure, flavours and aromas.

In addition to the variation in grapes and in the fortification processes used to make these wines, the method of ageing is a critical factor in VDN production. VDNs have traditionally been aged in an oxidative method, whereby the wines are put into barrels or large, wooden vats that are not entirely filled, so that oxygen can penetrate the wine. Some air also penetrates the containers, but the main oxidation comes from the air left inside with the wine.

The colours describing these wines derive from the colours of the land and houses in Roussillon; in addition to red, white and rosé, there are wines described as *garnet* (garnet), *ambré* (amber) and *tuilé*, this last being a wine whose colour is reminiscent of the orange tone of the curved, fired-clay roof tiles used on local buildings.

Some VDNs are placed in bonbons, which are large, rounded jars of 60, 70 or 80 litres. They are then left outside for up to a year to age in the shimmering heat of the summer and the chilly air of winter. There may be a grill or shelf above the wines to protect them from hail or falling branches in this very windy climate. The clear glass bonbon jars often have colourful caps of red, yellow or blue. It's quite startling to suddenly come upon a group of these brightly topped, giant jars filled with wine and lined up on an outdoor balcony or windowsill, or set out in rows in a field as if they were growing there.

The wine's development is dependent not only on temperature but on daylight as well. Both the structure and the colour of the wine are thus softened, resulting in added hues of blue, yellow, brown and even metallic glints; the result is the magically named *goût de lumière*, 'the taste of light'.

When the wine is brought in from the extremes of the weather, it needs to recover for a few years, and to be matured slowly and carefully in barrels of oak or chestnut, or other neutral containers, depending on the needs of each wine. The wine is often – but not always – blended before bottling. The finished wine will be a true marriage of the elements, and contain hints of leather, chocolate, candied orange peel and other appealing flavours and aromas.

Vins doux naturels are traditionally aged for at least several years before being released. Some are aged for decades. Each appellation has its own detailed requirements. For example, wines that are labelled *hors d'age* (very old) may be many decades old, and are not vintage designated. The youngest wines in these blends must be at least five years old. *Rancio* style wines are oxidized too, and must also have at least five years of ageing, but the wines will also have been aged for some of that time in extremes of heat and cold, and they must have specific dried fruit aromas and flavours. *Rancio* wines are made only in the AOP regions of Rivesaltes, Maury and Banyuls.

Certain appellation wines are not aged oxidatively. Instead they are aged in bottles or other glass containers to avoid contact with the air (oxygen) and the resultant oxidation.

In the 1980s the *rimage* style was developed by producers in Banyuls who wanted a somewhat fresher style of VDN. They also wanted their wine to project the characteristics of the vintage and of the terroir. *Rimage* wines are vintage dated. The wine is made from the highest-quality grapes from the best areas and best harvests. *Rimage mise précoce* is a further delineation of this style of wine, and it means that the wine is bottled very soon after vinification in order to emphasize its freshness and youth. This wine may be released after only six or eight months of ageing, which makes the grape selection even more critical. Banyuls is the only sub-region where the term *rimage* is used. However, this type of wine is also produced in Rivesaltes and Maury, where it is termed *grenat* (garnet).

As mentioned above, the first wines to receive the noteworthy French appellation status in the Roussillon region were the venerated, historic vins doux naturels. They received appellation status in 1936, the first year the wine appellation system was instituted throughout France. The first AOC (now the EU-standardized AOP designation) wines in Roussillon were AOC Rivesaltes, Banyuls and Maury. AOC Muscat de Rivesaltes dates from 1956, and the elevated AOC Banyuls Grand Cru was instituted in 1962.

Certain refinements were made or added to existing AOP des-ignations. In 1997 AOP Rivesaltes added the *ambré* and *tuilé* styles, and in 2002, the *grenat* style as well. In 2011 AOP Rivesaltes added a rosé definition, and Maury further defined its sweet wines as Maury Doux (Sweet), to be made in the following styles: *ambré*, *tuilé*, *grenat* and *blanc* (white).

Specific AOPs are defined by their geographic area and by which grapes can be used. Production methods and ageing requirements must also be met, and the finished wines must have certain organo-leptic qualities that are specified for each sub-region. Here are a few of the regulations for Roussillon's VDN AOP wines.

AOP Banyuls can be red (*rimage*), white, rosé, *ambré* or *tuilé* (also known as *traditionel*). AOP Banyuls Grand Cru can only be made using at least 75 per cent red Grenache grapes of the highest (*grand cru*) quality. It is made in the *muté sur grains* method. After pressing, the wine is then aged for at least thirty months in wood. Though it

Hillside vineyards outside a Roussillon village with typical ochre-coloured tile roofs. One of the styles of vin doux naturel is called *tuilé* after the colour of these roof tiles.

Vins doux naturels ageing outside in the elements, in their traditional, large glass *bonbon* containers, with brightly coloured caps.

The flavours and colours of vins doux naturels soften and darken as they age, as shown in the hues of this deep tawny wine.

is fortified, this wine occasionally finishes with a sugar content on the low side; if the residual sugar is up to 54 grams/litre it may be labelled 'dry', 'sec' or 'brut'.

AOP Maury Doux can be made as *ambré, tuilé, grenat* or white, using all three Grenache varieties as well as some of the additional grape varieties mentioned above. Ageing requirements range from minimums of eight to thirty months in different production manners.

AOP Muscat de Rivesaltes is always a white wine, unoxidized, and can only be made with the two types of Muscat grapes: Muscat à Petits Grains and/or Muscat of Alexandria. There is one special designation for Muscat de Noel (Christmas Muscat) wine, which can be released in time for the holidays during the year of harvest; otherwise no wine can be released until at least the first of February in the year after the harvest.

AOP Rivesaltes can be made with Grenache and other authorized grapes in the region, depending on the style chosen by the wine producer. Also depending on style, these wines must be aged for at least eight to thirty months, and many are aged for years or decades longer. There is one exception: the rosé, which must be bottled by 31 December in the year following the harvest – though it is sometimes bottled earlier to maintain the freshness expected with a rosé-style wine.

Extended-life Wines and How to Drink Them

When the wine merchants of Roussillon first started fortifying their wines, they did it mainly to make the wines more desirable as exports. Happily, the fortification and ageing processes that developed in Roussillon also had the effect of allowing the wines to last for decades longer than anyone had imagined. This is still true today and is important to know because it makes buying and storing vins doux naturels much simpler: these wines tend to retain their aromas and flavours for many, many years. After bottling, VDNs do not need to be aged any further; they are ready to drink when purchased – though they can be kept longer.

In the past winemakers always maintained stocks of wines that were ten, twenty, thirty or more years old for blending, but now that demand and production are down, some of these beautifully aged wines are being bottled and sold. So today it is still possible to purchase great vintages for celebrating notable birthdays and anniversaries.

Vins doux naturels have a range of sweetness, yet they also contain savoury elements that are more or less prominent, depending on the sub-region and style of the producer. Because of the duality in the taste of these wines – sweet yet salty – there are many ways to drink VDNs. In all instances, however, these wines are better when served lightly chilled. Not super-cold, but around 12–15°C (55–60°F). The wines are served in small white wine glasses. A typical serving is smaller than for table wines – about 100 ml (3 oz.). These wines are meant to be savoured in a leisurely manner.

Vins doux naturels were traditionally served as aperitifs. The wines are wonderful when sipped on their own before a meal. They can be paired with toasted or salted nuts, especially almonds. In the U.S., where cheese is often served as an appetizer, the wines can also be matched with chèvre and other tangy cheeses.

Today, VDNs are most often served after the meal. With their flavours of dried fruits encasing a piquant layer of fresh, mineral-and-iodine-scented seaside air, the wines' sweetness is balanced with lively acidity and strength. VDNs pair well with blue cheese, with nutty and caramel dishes, with dried fruits or fruit tarts, with the regional speciality *crème Catalane* – and the sweeter wines go especially well with chocolate cakes and other sweet dessert dishes.

In many circumstances, VDNs can take the place of either wines or spirits, adding an essence of thoughtfulness, and an appreciation of centuries of craft. There's no need to hesitate about opening a bottle for any occasion because the wine will stay fresh in the

From gold to ochre to garnet to dark amber, these are the colours of Roussillon's vins doux naturels, in a variety of ages.

Vignobles Terrassous' award-winning Rivesaltes vins doux naturels showing the gradations of colour achieved by ageing.

A swirl of ochre-amber vin doux naturel, its bright colour contrasting with the green garden.

refrigerator for many months, and remain lively through many distinctive food pairings.

It may be surprising to learn that, outside of Roussillon, very little VDN wine is consumed in France. Historically these wines were either regional specialities or they were exported. Currently, the U.S., Germany, Belgium, the UK, the Netherlands and Denmark have the most appreciative consumers of VDNs. However, nations as diverse as China, Switzerland and Lithuania are now catching up.

Vin Doux Naturel Expands in the Twentieth Century

During the twentieth century, a few additional regions in southern France officially began producing their own vins doux naturels. These areas are in the Languedoc and the southern Rhone, and on the island of Corsica. A main impetus was consumer demand, as well as the suitability of their terroir to the Grenache grape, which grows well on fairly desolate hillsides.

In the 1940s the VDN market expanded, echoing in part a population increase in France. Also, it was feasible to continue producing VDNs in many areas, despite any temporary economic and political slumps, because in the event of war or other catastrophes these wines did not need to be sold immediately: they age beautifully both before and after bottling.

Another major impetus for the new VDN producers was as response to a cataclysmic freeze that occurred in Provence and the southern Rhone areas in 1956. The region's prolific olive oil industry died out when the olive trees froze that year. At the same time, the cold forced the shepherds to take their sheep further downhill, abandoning the higher slopes. Both of these occurrences left the hillsides open for more vineyards to be planted; grapevines can weather the occasional touch of frost, even though the grape harvest may suffer a bit for a year.

VDN production did not appear randomly in these additional appellations. For some time, a small amount of sweet and fortified wines had been made in these areas by producers that were inspired by Roussillon's great wines. In the Rhone the winemakers of Rasteau made their first commercial vintage in 1934, mainly made with Grenache Noir ('black' or red grenache) grapes, along with some Grenache Gris (grey) and Grenache Blanc (white) grapes. It wasn't until 1944 that Rasteau's VDN wines were awarded AOC status, retroactive to the 1943 vintage.

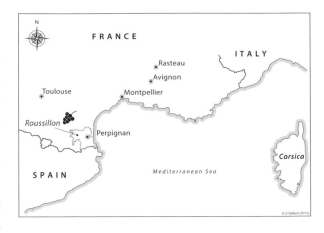

Originally, the amber-coloured vins doux naturels were called *doré* (golden) in Rasteau. Today, the VDN wines of Rasteau essentially follow the same production styles as those of Roussillon: *ambré* (instead of doré), *tuilé*, *rancio* and *hors d'age* (sixty months in the oxidative ageing process). The wines themselves can be white, rosé or *grenat* ('garnet' or red). While VDNs make up only 4 per cent of the production of Rasteau, winemakers there are still very proud of their 75-year heritage of sweet wine production.

Many wine consumers in Rasteau originally looked to VDNs as their aperitif before dinner. However, their grandmothers were likely to have taken a small glass after lunch, with sweet biscuits or cookies. Today, the consumption of VDNs has become much more of a speciality for wine connoisseurs who now sip it after dinner, with (or instead of) dessert. Most of the Rasteau VDN wines are now consumed locally. Little is exported, in part owing to the higher taxes which are added onto these little-known fortified wines. Rasteau's minimum alcohol percentage is 15 per cent, which is in line with other VDNs.

The world-famous Muscat de Beaumes-de-Venise AOP region is also in the Rhone Valley. Its location is northeast of the city of Avignon, a little south of Rasteau. Though Muscat wines have been grown on terraces there for centuries, even millennia, this wine

A light drink in the afternoon: a glass of Muscat de Saint-Jean-de-Minervois.

received its AOC designation for VDNs only in 1945 (retroactive to the 1943 vintage).

Muscat de Beaumes-de-Venise VDN wines must have a minimum of 15 per cent alcohol, which makes them quite appealing and easier to drink than some of the fortified wines made elsewhere. The wines are produced with both Muscat à Petits Grains Blanc (white) and Noir ('black' or red). Depending on the grapes used, the finished wines may be amber, rosé or even dark purple in colour. These wines are produced in very limited amounts, and are prized by connoisseurs.

The situation is not that different in other VDN-producing areas of southern France, in terms of production and consumption. And there are only a few other areas that make these wines. One is Corsica, which produces a VDN called Muscat du Cap-Corse that has had its AOP designation only since 1993. Closer to Roussillon, in Languedoc, there are four more VDN AOPs: Muscat de Frontignan dating from 1936; Muscat de Lunel since 1943; Muscat de Saint-Jean-de-Minervois since 1949; and Muscat de Mireval since 1959. These are all specialized, small-production wines in their areas. These wines are made with one grape, Muscat à Petits Grains Blanc.

A Snapshot of Vin Doux Naturel Today

For centuries, Roussillon produced around 80 per cent VDNs and 20 per cent table wines. In just the last few decades consumer taste has undergone such a profound change that these percentages are now essentially reversed. The lion's share of wine produced in Roussillon is now red and white table wine.

By the end of the twentieth century, a decreasing demand for sweet wines was slowly taking its toll on the VDN industry in Roussillon – just as it was in other fortified wine production areas of the world. The *caves cooperatives* (wine co-ops) that were the result of the Catalan peasants' revolt in the early 1900s remained critical to the local wine industry throughout most of the twentieth century. However, in the twenty-first century, for economies of scale, and to accommodate the shift in consumer wine demand, many of Roussillon's wine cooperatives have merged into much larger entities. Today those co-ops that remain are quite active and lively. L'Etoile in Banyuls is one of the most well-known as it is located in a lovely area at the seaside in Banyuls-sur-Mer, easy for tourists to wander into. It is a great source for dry as well as sweet wines, with tastings offered on the premises as well. Another group of cooperatives merged and renamed itself after the inventor of fortified wines, Arnaud de Villeneuve. This group has four wineries, and a beautifully designed large shop and tasting area in the historic centre of the inland town of Rivesaltes. In addition to selling wines, they offer vineyard and winery tours along with tastings.

There are cooperatives of different types and sizes in other Roussillon towns too. They produce table wines as well as VDNs of all types. They also pay attention to design and marketing for their wines. And they have a historical advantage: storerooms of inestimably valuable barrels full of beautifully aged vin doux naturel going back a hundred years. These are wines which can be bottled as needed. So the cooperatives have become great resources for cele-bratory, anniversary and holiday wines, carrying both long-aged VDNs and newer, dry and sweet wines.

Though white and red table wines are responsible for the majority of wine sales in Roussillon today, winemakers there are committed to continuing to produce their rare and wonderful VDNs. Slowly, ever so slowly, vin doux naturel is being rediscovered by consumers ranging from holidayers to wine directors. Sommeliers in locations as diverse as New York City and Hong Kong are falling

A simple, refreshing aperitif: vin doux naturel over ice, with a slice of lemon.

Bright, graphic labels for young vins doux naturels attract consumers of all ages.

Modern graphics and decanter-like bottles attract new consumers while signifying respect for quality in these esteemed, older vintages of Terrassous' Rivesaltes vins doux naturels.

in love with this 'salted caramel wine'. It is happening beyond the big international cities, too: wine directors from Michigan and Manchester are putting these wines on their menus in by-the-glass and tasting-flight-sized offerings – and even offering VDN-based cocktails to their discerning customers.

7
Worldwide
Fortified Wines

Fortified wines can be made in any area that grows wine grapes and has access to distillation. Historically, at times fortification has acted as a preservation agent for wine, while in other instances it has allowed unremarkable wines to shine in new iterations.

For the past 8,000 years various civilizations have been using additives to make their wines more enjoyable. Ancient cultures learned that anything from water to honey to herbs and spices could solve the problem of an overly strong wine, a weak wine, or a lesser quality wine, by adding enticing aromas and flavours. Adding alcohol (fortifying a wine) also improves its ageing potential.

Looking at fortified wines from the perspective of the early twenty-first century, there are as many new, stimulating stories of classics reborn as there are tales of woe about declining awareness. Some wines are on an upswing in popularity, and others are just experiencing the barest stirrings of rejuvenation. This is a global chronicle, both past and present.

Some well-known fortified wines are being duplicated and shamelessly labelled as originals in other parts of the world. However, in most of the better wine regions, producers have begun using labels that clearly identify the style of wine without attempting to deceive their customers.

There is also a small coterie of original wines that have star value in their own regions, but have not made the leap to international commercial success. These are fortified wines that were created in one small region, where they have been in continuous production for decades, even centuries. Visitors find the wines as delightful as do the inhabitants, yet the wines remain sequestered for some reason, appreciated only in their home territories.

Popular and Prestigious

For centuries, fortified wines have proved popular around the world. The most successful of them have been valued more highly abroad than in their home regions. Sometimes this was because they were shipped to regions where grapes couldn't be grown; sometimes it was because of the prestige the wines gathered and created. Either way, they have captivated consumers in countless countries for many centuries. Once the process of fortifying wine became common knowledge in the late Middle Ages, one might wonder why it was only a certain half-dozen wines that became – and remained – famous.

For that matter, why didn't winemakers all over the world make fortified wines? The simple answer is that they did. And they still do. Knowledge of wine fortification broadened as European populations spread around the globe, inspiring winemakers in far-flung corners of the globe to produce their own fortified wines. Some of these local wines became extremely popular in their home countries. However, they were generally playing second fiddle to existing famous wines with decades of sterling reputations, as well as long-established commercial activity, behind them.

Port, sherry, Madeira, Marsala, vermouth and vin doux naturel: all were distinctive stars of their own regions. Many wine producers have attempted to imitate them. Some of the imitations have faded into lower-quality products of generic sameness. But others – notably vermouths – are lively and growing in popularity now, often inspired by the intense curiosity of the current generation of winemakers at home, and of wine directors and mixologists around the world.

New Versions of Traditional Wines

A few of the most intrepid sommeliers seem to have rediscovered the great French vin doux naturel sweet wines, and some of these wines are now popping up on restaurant wine lists in diverse, global cities wherever they can be imported from France. There are no well-known imitators of the French vins doux naturels, and that may simply be an artefact of the present era. The situation is similar with regard to both Marsala and Madeira wines: small numbers of intrepid consumers and sommeliers are keeping the wines current. Though wine aficionados and people in the wine trade have long appreciated these wines, most wine-drinkers know little about them.

Nevertheless, in the vin doux naturel area in the south of France, as well as in Madeira and in Marsala, there's a novel splash of elegant, wonderful wines, both dry and sweet, now being produced by both traditional and new wineries. It's only a matter time before the trending increase in global tourism prompts visitors to bring back these fresh wines as souvenirs of their trips; the next step is for people to request them at restaurants and wine shops at home, the same way so many other wines have achieved popularity outside their native regions.

Vermouth is having the opposite experience: there are more new vermouth innovators around the world than can be counted, with additional producers appearing constantly. Inspired both by cocktail artists and European culturists, vermouth's popularity has surged in recent decades. Vermouth di Torino in Italy has taken steps to protect its origins and requirements with the 'di Torino' label. Elsewhere, the sky's the limit in terms of production methods and herbal additives. Wine producers are seeking out the clearest, most lively methods of distilling herbs to add to their fortified wines. Each wine region has its own, native-grown grapes to use for its wine base. Finished vermouths can be sweet or dry, red or white; there's something to appeal to every palate. It's impossible to predict how intensely this explosive movement will develop. More fun is yet to come, as individual bars in different countries are even producing their own vermouths. The latest trend circles around to replicate an older tradition: vermouth on tap, from the barrel.

What the Names Mean

Since the inception of the European Union, naming conflicts have escalated around the world, with some still unresolved. In the New World (non-European regions) locally made fortified wines were originally produced simply to supply inhabitants with popular beverages at reasonable prices – without the costs associated with importing the originals. The New World versions were often labelled with the same names as their European originals, especially port and sherry. In recent decades, reacting to pressure from the original denominations of origin, New World producers first began to label their products 'sherry-style wines' or 'port-style wines' instead of 'sherry' or 'port'. Later, wine producers in some countries chose entirely new names for their products. In other instances, producers have refused to change their labelling – though these are fortunately in the minority, most often involving lower-quality products that require the stolen cachet for sales.

Within the European Union, each country or wine region that requests it may be granted sole use of one particular name for their wine or grape – after considerable debate, of course. In the instance of port and sherry, there was little debate in the EU because there was little port-style or sherry-style wine made outside of their home regions in Portugal and Spain. But outside of the EU, each wine region and/or country has had to negotiate their own agreement not to use an EU term for their wines, requiring dozens of finely crafted settlements. Needless to say, this process has not always gone smoothly, and not every wine region has signed agreements with each EU region. Some of the negotiations have taken decades, with the producers becoming pawns in much larger diplomatically motivated trade and tariff negotiations between countries.

Wines By Style

To further complicate matters in consumer labelling, each country or region has the right to develop their own method for labelling, once they agree to not use the European denomination of origin terms on their local wine labels. With dozens of producers in each region poised to protect their own livelihoods as well as their regional history, the politics of crafting a new label is never simple.

One way of indicating a wine's similarity to a type and style of European fortified wine is to use a labelling term that implies the style of the wine, such as 'tawny' for port-style wines. In South Africa producers are now using identifiers such as 'vintage', 'tawny' and 'ruby' for their port-style wines – but they do not add the word 'port'. Also, because they feel that the word 'Cape' is identified with South Africa, producers there have the option to add the word 'Cape' on the label, as in 'Cape Tawny'.

A similar tactic has been chosen for South African sherry-style wines; however, they have been less successful in getting compliance from local producers, especially those that produce inexpensive sweet wines. In South Africa, the dry sherry-style wines are meant to be labelled 'pale' and the sweet ones 'cream'. 'Cream' producers can add additional descriptors, and phrases such as 'medium cream' and 'full cream' are used to indicate levels of sweetness. But overall, many suppliers still refer to their fortified wine categories as 'sherry-style' or 'port-style' wines.

Australian producers of port-style wines are taking the same approach as the South Africans, labelling their wines with the traditional port-style terms 'vintage' and 'tawny' but omitting the word 'port' – and they seem to be much more effective at implementing these labelling guidelines.

New Names

Going in another direction, Australian producers of sherry-style wines have opted for
a new term altogether. 'Apera' is the current
name for Australia's sherry-style wines.
Producers seem quite happy to have a new
term for these fortified wines. Though there
has always been a reliable market for their
Australian-made sherry-style wines, they felt
that many consumers had developed mis-

Campbells, one of
Australia's original premier
wine producers, currently
makes several versions
of extremely popular
fortified wines.

taken impressions, often viewing sherry solely as an old-fashioned,
sweet beverage. So apera producers have welcomed the chance to
introduce new generations to their fine (mainly) dry fortified wines.

Australia also has its own famous sweet fortified wines.
Rutherglen Muscat wines are produced in only one wine region in
northeast Victoria. The wines are uniquely made with a red grape,
the rare Muscat à Petits Grains Rouge. Producers of this wine have
a long history of prize-winning wines in the Rutherglen area. In
the same region winemakers also produce a fortified wine with the
Muscadelle grape. This wine is called Topaque or Liqueur Topaque.
Until recently this wine was known as Tokay, before an agreement
was reached with Hungarian Tokaji producers who objected to other
regions' labels that used the word 'Tokaj' or 'Tokay'.

In the U.S. one producer of port-style wines decided early on to
meet the new EU-motivated labelling challenge with humour. Quady,
based in Madera, California, calls its port-style wines 'Starboard' and
has achieved great success with this name for decades.

Pockets of Riches

Throughout the wine world, there are nuggets of locally treasured
fortified wines to discover, and Italy is a prime example – though
no doubt there are similar situations in Spain, France, Greece and

other winemaking countries. For example, Aleatico di Gradoli is a historic fortified wine made traditionally in the central Italian Lazio province – a wine that is little known outside this region. In Trentino, there is a wine producer who recently decided to use a brandy he had made to fortify his own wine, naming it Pojer e Sandri Merlino Rosso Fortificato Vigneti delle Dolomiti IGT.

During the 1990s, several winemakers in the Veneto began to produce a fortified version of the Recioto della Valpolicella wine. It was not part of the official regional denominational wine (it was not qualified to carry DOC or DOCG designation) and production soon lapsed. However, at least one winemaker is starting up production again now.

Sardinia has its own long tradition of fortified wines, dating back to the 1300s, when the very first fortified wines in the world were produced. Currently, production centres on fortified Vernaccia wine, which is made in both dry and sweet versions. This grape and the wine are called Vernaccia di Oristano. The wine is aged in barrels under flor (a particular type of yeast that forms a fluffy layer on the wine, as in the sherry wines of Jerez). It is aged in a solera system – again, like sherry. Very few people outside of Sardinia are familiar with this fortified wine, but it is such an integral element

Water is so scarce on the Mediterranean island of Pantelleria that the grapevines must grow low enough to the ground to capture the dew for moisture. But they produce a heavenly fortified wine.

The important Massandra winery with a bust of Prince Lev Golitsyn, a founder of wine production in the Crimea.

of Sardinia's cultural history that Vernaccia di Oristano was the first Sardinian wine to receive DOC status, in 1971.

The Sardinian firm of Sella & Mosca specializes in reviving traditions in Sardinian wine. Currently, the most famous modern Sardinian fortified wine is Sella & Mosca's Anghelu Ruju, which is made with dried Cannonau grapes; Cannonau is the Sardinian term for Grenache.

On Pantelleria, an island near Tunisia that is actually part of Italy, there is a fortified Zibibbo wine called Moscato di Pantelleria; Zibibbo is the local name for the Muscat of Alexandria grape. The Sicily-based winery Donnafugata has popularized an excellent version of this wine under the romantic label Ben Ryé, which means 'son of the wind'.

As mentioned before, examples can be taken from many regions and many countries. There is one more to reveal now, because it is a singular wine, rarely tasted outside its home region of Crimea. The famed Massandra winery was established there by Tsar Nicholas II in 1894, on the shores of the Black Sea. He built it to supply wines to the nearby summer palaces of Russia's royal families. In the succeeding 120 years Massandra has been co-opted by many different regimes and governments, but through it all it has retained its impressive reputation for producing sweet, fortified wines of royal significance. A large proportion of the wine is made in the style of port and sherry. Many of the wines are said to mature only after forty, fifty or even sixty years of ageing. The winery also produces non-fortified wines; some are dry but most are dessert wines that are highly respected in Russia and the former Soviet countries. Massandra wines are not currently exported, though some older bottles occasionally become available, especially in the UK.

Four Historic Gems

A few of the most significant, historic fortified wines from different regions are more than worthy of discussion here: Moscatel de Setúbal and Carcavelos from near Lisbon in Portugal, Commandaria from southern Cyprus, and Mavrodaphne from the Peloponnese and Cefalù in Greece.

To begin, it is significant that one of the most notable grapes used in fortified wines has had a difficult time of it in the U.S. and in some other countries: the Muscat grape, which is also known as Moscatel. At some point in the twentieth century, this grape name became synonymous with a cheap sweet drink labelled 'Muscatel' in America. Elsewhere, Moscatel wines were also some of the lowest-level wines produced, especially for Iberian populations at home and in the former colonies. Sometimes the drinks labelled Muscatel and Moscatel weren't actually wines at all. They were merely fortified juice (presumably grape juice) sold very cheaply – the types of bottles that were seen clutched in brown bags by down-and-out populations on the sidewalks of big cities in the U.S. Because of this, any wine now labelled 'Moscatel' has a long way to go to earn back its reputation.

This is especially unfortunate when it comes to great fortified wines like those from Portugal's Moscatel de Setúbal DOC (*Denominação de Origem Controlada*) region. There are barely half a dozen remaining producers of this wine in this denominated region near Lisbon. Nevertheless, those few are dedicated not only to continuing production, but to polishing their processes and improving their wines. For example, both the nearly-two-hundred-year-old company José Maria da Fonseca and the much newer Malo winery (established in the year 2000) produce wines made with the rare red Muscat grape Moscatel Roxo, as well as with the more conventional white Muscat of Alexandria grape. They have each refined their fortification techniques by using spirits from Armagnac and Cognac to fortify their wines in order to create more sophisticated products, suitable for a worldwide market. José Maria da Fonseca also has the advantage of an incredible array of historic Moscatel de Setúbal wines, which they invite visitors to taste, opening bottles of different vintages of the wines in convenient Enomatic wine-preserving machines.

Even rarer is Portugal's Carcavelos wine, which has only one remaining producer today: Villa Oeiras. This villa was the hunting estate of the Marquis de Pombal, a man who has been celebrated in the area since the mid-eighteenth century because of his success in rebuilding the city of Lisbon after its catastrophic 1755 earthquake. (Pombal was also responsible for innovations in port, which is made further north in Portugal.) With the marquis' influence, the fortified wines of Carcavelos – some of which were made on his estate – became well known and remained luxury wines for over 150 years.

Slanting sun colours the entrance to the famed Setúbal winery José Maria da Fonseca, which is nearly 200 years old.

The 18th-century house of the Marquis de Pombal, which he used as a hunting lodge, outside the city of Lisbon. He also made wine on the estate, and today the building and surrounding vineyards are the last remaining estate-made Carcavelos DOC fortified wines.

The wine cellar for the Carcavelos DOC fortified wines made on the former estate of the Marquis de Pombal, near Lisbon.

After the last of the marquis' descendants departed Villa Oeiras in the early decades of the twentieth century, the estate was acquired by an investor who started selling off tracts of land to build apartments for Lisbon's expanding population. In the 1990s the final parcel of Carcavelos DOC vineyard land was set to be sold off for housing. Just in time, the municipality of Oeiras and the Portuguese government teamed up and acquired the Marquis de Pombal's villa along with the last remaining vineyards of his original estate, to honour the marquis' contributions in Portuguese history. The villa and barns were then used for offices as well as for a winery. Currently, the government employs winemakers to continue making the historic Carcavelos DOC fortified wines.

Though the other Carcavelos estates have stopped producing wines, having sold off their vineyards to housing developers, there are a few – such as Quinta da Bela Vista and Quinta do Barão – that still bottle and sell their remaining stocks of Carcavelos DOC wine. However, rumour has it that there may be enough tiny vineyard parcels left intact for one of these wineries to start producing a little more Carcavelos again.

A legendary wine whose antecedents date to biblical times, Commandaria is produced on the Mediterranean island of Cyprus. Its name derives from the location where the wine has been made for nine hundred years: the 'central command' castle built by the Knights Templar after King Richard the Lionheart of England invaded the island in AD 1192. Following this, there was a surge in demand for 'Commandaria' wine, which had garnered a sterling reputation early on, allegedly at one of the world's first wine competitions, held early in the thirteenth century. The wine was especially prized by citizens of the Serene Republic of Venice for several centuries. At some point in this period, Commandaria also began to be produced as a fortified wine.

In 1571 the Ottoman Sultan Selim II conquered Cyprus, allegedly for the wine, which he apparently thoroughly enjoyed though he was ostensibly a Muslim. After his reign, under Ottoman rule Commandaria production and export all but died out owing to religious/cultural prohibitions on drinking alcohol.

A few centuries later, Cyprus came under British protection and then rule from 1878 to 1959. At that point Commandaria had basically been reduced to local consumption. In 1960, the year after Cyprus gained its freedom, the first Commandaria wine cooperatives were formed to improve both the quality and quantity of the wine, and production increased for a number of years. There was a dip in production when the Turkish invaded Cyprus in 1974. The Turks ended up occupying only the northern third of the island, while the southern section – including the fourteen villages that comprise the Commandaria production area – have remained under the control of

One of the oldest continuously produced fortified wines, an award-winner for centuries, this is Cyprus' famed Commandaria wine.

Greek-ancestry Cypriots, who have no prohibition on alcohol. After things settled down, increased exports to the USSR motivated a production upsurge until the Soviet republics disbanded in 1991.

During the ensuing decades, production quantity and quality have been uneven. However, worldwide, this wine retains the stellar historical reputation it has had since the Middle Ages. Cypriots today are hoping to re-energize Commandaria by taking steps towards producing a more consistent, quality product and by creating more awareness in the wine world.

Commandaria wine is made with either the white Xynisteri grape or the red Mavro grape (no relation to the Greek Mavrodaphne), or a blend of Xynisteri and Mavro in any proportion. The grapes are harvested late in the season, for optimum ripeness and sugar content. Then they are spread out on mats in the sun to dry, in order to further concentrate the grape sugars and flavours before pressing. After a long, slow natural fermentation, the wine is aged in oak barrels for a minimum of two years. Sometimes the wine is fortified and sometimes not; it's the producer's choice.

Often, Commandaria is aged in a modified solera system called *mana* (or *manna*), where the wine barrels are never fully emptied of their aged wines before the new wines are added. The barrels can also be 'sealed' at any time, so the remaining wine will continue to age for additional years or even decades longer. Reports of hundred-year-old wines appear periodically – though when an age is given for Commandaria, it is not always clear whether the age refers to the vintage of the wine or the date of the inception of the solera. Either way, this venerable wine excels in complexity, aromas, flavours and balanced sweetness. Only extremely small amounts of this wine are bottled and released every year, so Commandaria's legendary character is also enhanced by its rarity.

Though Mavrodaphne is one of the most famous wines of Greece, it was created by a Bavarian named Gustav Clauss. Clauss settled in Greece in 1854 and built a winery in Patras, the capital city of the Peloponnese. He planted his own vineyards in 1861. In 1873

The arid region of Cyprus where Commandaria is produced; Commandaria wines have been winning awards for centuries.

A view of one of the cellars at the winery Achaia Clauss, where Gustav Clauss invented the fortified wine Mavrodaphne in Greece in the mid-19th century. Mavrodaphne's fame quickly spread throughout the world and it is still well known today.

he created his Mavrodaphne wine, a dark purple, sweet, fortified wine that he is said to have named after the beautiful, dark eyes of his fiancée, who sadly died before they could be married. With that wine (and that heartbreaking story) Clauss built a business of producing and exporting his wines, which have become well known throughout Europe. Today his winery, Achaia Clauss, continues to produce both dry and sweet wines in Patras.

Mavrodaphne wine from Patras, Greece, became so well known around the world that labels were apparently printed not just in the original Greek but in other languages. This elaborate, historical German version advises that Mavrodaphne wine is good for everything from dessert to medicine.

In Greek, the word *mavro* means black. Mavrodaphne grapes are considered 'black', a grape colour that is usually described as 'red' in English. To produce the wine, the grapes are harvested late and semi-dried to concentrate their aromas, flavours and sugars. After a short period of fermentation, the young wine is fortified with neutral spirit. The resulting higher-alcohol wine is then aged in oak. PDO Mavrodaphne of Patras must be aged in oak barrels for a year. 'Reserve' wines must be aged for two years in oak and one in the bottle. In order to carry the designation 'Grand Reserve' the wines must be aged for seven years.

Mavrodaphne of Patras became a PDO (Protected Designation of Origin) wine in 1971. Mavrodaphne of Patras continues to be incredibly popular in Greece. Currently, there are about two dozen wineries producing this wine. In that same year the fortified sweet wine Mavrodaphne of Cefalonia wine also received PDO status. The Mavrodaphne grapes grown on the island of Cefalù are a different clone from those of Patras, but the production method is the same. This wine has become extremely rare even on Cefalù, with only four wineries currently producing it. Interestingly, some grapes grown on the nearby island of Ithaca can also be included in PDO Mavrodaphne of Cefalonia.

Every region that makes wines has its own versions of these stories: wines that are – or were – historically or locally famous. In addition, new and established wineries in various regions are looking to expand wine consumers' palates and experiences. To this end, wineries are producing both innovative and traditional versions of fortified wines. New fortified wines may be produced in minute quantities, so it's best to seize the opportunity to taste one whenever it comes along.

Cocktail Recipes

Fortified wines form the basis of many classic cocktail recipes, especially vermouth, which has been used in the U.S. for over a hundred years. Other wines are newer to this style of imbibing, and creative mixologists are playfully inventing new ways to appreciate the depth and complexity of flavours. Sherries, for instance, are unsung heroes, contributing subtly and significantly to many mixed drinks today.

Many fortified wines make great summer drinks – a fun fact that is being discovered by consumers in various parts of the world who now enjoy unpretentious, refreshing long drinks of any of the sweeter fortified wines, mixed with tonic and served over ice. Here is a range of drink recipes from classic to postmodern, from exotic to extremely simple.

Vermouth

Vermouth is a quintessential element of many of the most famous classic cocktails. A Martini cannot be made without vermouth. Neither can a Manhattan. Or a Negroni, for that matter. Martinis and Manhattans, originating in America, have been popular around the world for the last century; Negronis are native to Italy, but are now being discovered by legions of discerning imbibers across the globe.

Martini

The Martini has evolved from a cocktail made with half gin and half vermouth, to less and less vermouth, to using vodka as the drink's base instead of gin. Trends have also morphed from using bianco to extra dry vermouth – and less and less vermouth altogether. The extreme Martini of the twenty-first century finally became simply a well-chilled pour of vodka, with the vermouth hovering near (but not in) the drink. Now the pendulum is swinging back a bit, driven by the recent availability of increasing numbers of high-quality vermouths.

In a Martini, popular additives such as olives, olive juice from the bottle, twists of lemon, dashes of bitters – even ice – are all optional, depending on individual preference. The recipe? Start at one end of the spectrum, balancing one style of vermouth with a choice of gin or vodka. Then proceed to the opposite end of the vermouth spectrum until your perfect balance is found.

Manhattan

The Manhattan cocktail originated, of course, in New York City. Originally, it was made with American rye whiskey. Today it is also often bourbon-based. Here's a simple, classic formula.

60 ml (2 oz.) rye or bourbon
30 ml (1 oz.) red vermouth
1 dash Angostura bitters

Add ingredients to chilled ice-filled mixing glass and stir well. Strain into glass and garnish with a Maraschino or brandied cherry.

Negroni

A classic of Northern Italy, where enticingly bitter herbal drinks are timeless and sophisticated. The Negroni is served as an aperitif, to awaken the appetite and stimulate new energy for the evening.

30 ml (1 oz.) London dry gin
30 ml (1 oz.) Campari
30 ml (1 oz.) red vermouth

Add ingredients to chilled mixing glass and stir well. Strain into ice-filled glass and serve. Optional garnish: twist of orange zest.

Port

While a glass of port is often simply sipped after dinner – without anything added – port has also long been a major component of punches, which were extremely popular in the UK and U.S. from as early as the eighteenth century. Port was also used as a basis for drinks when the American cocktail movement was getting its start in the mid-nineteenth century. In the twenty-first century, port has been making a slow but steady comeback in the mixology world.

Port Tonic

One of the simplest cocktails to make is the long drink called Port Tonic. This is often sipped by port producers at the end of a hot day in the vineyards of the Douro Valley. In Portugal this drink is most popularly made with white port. In other areas, young ruby ports and even the new rosé ports are also used. This drink is a success at full-strength as well as half-strength.

30–50 ml (1–2 oz.) port – white or other
young port
tonic

Splash port into a tall glass with ice. Top with tonic. Stir lightly. Optional garnish: add slice of orange or orange zest.

Next Step

This is a slightly more involved version of a Port Tonic, which is where the name 'Next Step' comes from. Today, almost anything can be served in a large, fun Martini glass; the trick is in mixing a balanced drink using unconventional ingredients. This drink plays to the strength of port's sweet side, counteracting it with the tanginess of tart cherry and fresh orange.

60 ml (2 oz.) Warre's Warrior Port
30 ml (1 oz.) vodka
15 ml (½ oz.) tart cherry juice
60–90 ml (2–3 oz.) tonic
½ orange slice

Stir port, vodka and cherry juice with ice in a mixing glass. Strain into large Martini glass with ice. Top with tonic. Twist orange before floating on drink to release oils and a few drops of juice.

Bar Drake Manhattan

Here is a classic of the cocktail world – the Manhattan – re-invented by mixologist and historian David Wondrich for Kobrand, a major u.s. port importer. Wondrich uses Fonseca Bin 27 Ruby Port as a basis for constructing this drink, skewing it towards port's innately luscious fruitiness. This version of the Manhattan is based on a drink from San Francisco's historic Sir Francis Drake Hotel, with a couple of small but important flourishes that tie the drink's flavours together: a lick of maple syrup and a garnish of brandied cherries.

65 ml (2¼ oz.) Woodford Reserve Bourbon
30 ml (1 oz.) Fonseca Bin 27 Ruby Port
1 barspoon (5 ml) maple syrup
1 dash Angostura bitters
brandied cherries

Pour ingredients over ice in mixing glass. Stir and strain into cocktail glass. Garnish with brandied cherries.

Sherry

Sherry began its popularity on the cocktail circuit in a simple drink – the Cobbler – that probably originated with home entertaining, as early as the eighteenth century. By the mid-1800s it was so popular that Charles Dickens even mentions it in one of his novels.

The Sherry Cobbler is simply a tall drink made with sherry stirred with sugar, poured over ice and garnished with fruit and sometimes herbs. Amontillado is often used because it has hints of nuttiness and vanilla, allowing the cocktail to feel either somewhat sweeter or more dry, depending on the individual amontillado chosen, as well as the rest of the ingredients. Here are three modern Cobblers.

Sherry Cobbler

60 ml (2 oz.) amontillado sherry
7.5 ml (¼ oz.) simple syrup
½ orange slice

Add ice to cocktail shaker. Add ingredients and shake energetically. Strain drink into glass filled with crushed ice. Garnish with half-slice of orange.

Note: the amount of simple syrup may be adjusted depending on the sweetness of the sherry.

Autumn Cobbler

The new UK-based sherry company XECO has plenty of experience making cobblers. They like using seasonal fruits to complement their amontillado sherry. The Autumn Cobbler is an adventure in orchards and hedgerows.

50 ml (1¾ oz.) amontillado sherry
25 ml (¾ oz.) lime juice
15 ml (½ oz.) simple syrup
120–250 ml (½–1 cup) autumnal fruit such as figs, pears,
pomegranates, damson, quince, etc. – peeled and cubed where
necessary

Muddle half the fruit in the bottom of a highball glass. Add rest of ingredients, fill with ice and stir. Garnish with rest of fruit.

Spring Cobbler

For a more summery feel, this cocktail is full of fresh berries and other warm-weather flavours – which also pair well with xeco amontillado. Nowadays fresh berries are available any time of the year, so this drink can be made even at the first whisper of spring.

50 ml (1¾ oz.) amontillado sherry
25 ml (¾ oz.) lime juice
15 ml (½ oz.) simple syrup
120–250 ml (½–1 cup) strawberries, raspberries or other
available summer fruit
2 thin orange slices
several mint leaves
1 thin wedge of lime

Lightly muddle half the fruit (except lime) in the bottom of a highball glass with mint. Add rest of ingredients, fill with ice and stir. Garnish with rest of fruit, lime and another mint leaf.

Madeira

Though Madeira wine ranges in style from dry to sweet, it has traditionally been served as a sipping drink. Very recently, Madeira producers have begun to look at using their wines in cocktails – and local as well as international mixologists have jumped at the chance to enter contests using Madeira to add dimension to their drinks.

Madeira Gold

This refreshing, deceptively simple drink is now served as the official cocktail of the presidency of the Regional Government of Madeira. It was created by Madeira mixologist Cesár Figueira, winner of Madeira's 2018 Cocktail Competition – a competition designed by the Association of Bartenders of Madeira to commemorate the 600th anniversary of the establishment of the island of Madeira as a region of Portugal.

50 ml (1¾ oz.) Madeira wine – five-year, dry
30 ml (1 oz.) orange liqueur
10 ml (⅓ oz.) fig liqueur
50 ml (1 ¾ oz.) zero-sugar fizzy lemonade
orange zest

Place ice cubes in shaker. Add Madeira wine, orange and fig liqueur. Shake well. Pour into tall glass over ice. Top with lemonade. Garnish with orange zest.

Caipimadeira

This take on a Caipirinha comes from Madeira Vintners, a new Madeira producer on the island, staffed by young people (mainly women), with a twenty-first-century attitude. Here is their version, made with a young, fairly dry Madeira wine.
Serves 4

1 lime
1 tablespoon sugar
240 ml (8 oz.) Madeira Vintners Fenix Seco
(or other dry, young Madeira wine)
240 ml (8 oz.) Sprite
mint leaves

Cut the lime into quarters and muddle with the sugar. Add the Madeira and Sprite. Divide among 4 large glasses filled with ice. Garnish with mint leaves.

Madeira Zest

Here is a simple, versatile drink that can be served sweet or dry, depending on the Madeira wine at hand, and the preference of the imbiber.

60 ml (2 oz.) Madeira wine, moderately dry or sweet, as preferred
tonic
lemon zest
Optional garnishes: fresh mint for sweeter drinks,
fresh thyme sprigs for drier cocktails

Pour Madeira into a tall glass over ice. Stir to chill. Top with tonic. Twist lemon zest before adding it. Stir lightly. Garnish as desired.

Marsala

While not traditionally used in cocktails, recent mixologists search-ing for new, stimulating ingredients have discovered different Marsala wines to add to their drinks. Marsala producers have also begun to offer cocktails to winery visitors and to feature cocktail recipes on their websites.

The Lost Sailor

From the Colombo Marsala Company, this 'not-so' Negroni is com-plex in flavour and intended to be sipped slowly. The sweet Colombo Marsala wine offsets the bitterness of the Italian Campari, emulating the taste of the classic Italian Negroni cocktail.

45 ml (1½ oz.) sweet Marsala wine
45 ml (1½ oz.) Campari
45 ml (1½ oz.) gin
orange zest

Combine ingredients in mixing glass with ice. Strain into cocktail glass over ice. Garnish with twisted orange zest.

150

The Florio Marsala company serves a cocktail called the 150, which is dedicated to the 150th anniversary of the unification of Italy. Marsala – and Florio in particular – figured in the original campaign to unite Italy in the mid-1800s.

60 ml (2 oz.) Vecchio Florio Marsala
45 ml (1½ oz.) elderflower cordial
4 mint leaves
sparkling water

Muddle mint leaves with elderflower cordial in a tall glass. Add ice and Marsala. Stir lightly. Top with sparkling water.

Star Ice Tea

This drink takes advantage of the spice and tea-like flavours in dry Marsala wine. Adding ginger and raspberries to the mix brings out the similarities as well as the contrasts, and combines them into a cocktail that is refreshingly dry.

60 ml (2 oz.) dry Marsala wine
30 ml (1 oz.) double-strength, brewed black tea
30 ml (1 oz.) ginger ale
1 piece star anise
4 fresh raspberries

Mix Marsala and tea. Pour over a single ice cube in a coupe glass. Top with ginger ale. Float star anise in drink. Add raspberry garnish.

Vin Doux Naturel

Though VDNs have not traditionally been used in cocktails, they do contain critical elements of fruit and acidity as well as added depth owing to the vinification processes of the finished wines. Some of the younger VDNs lend themselves quite easily to cocktails. The older wines range in colour from amber to brick orange, garnet and purple, which adds another dimension to the drink.

Riv'Tonic

A simple summer drink that's not too sweet, and carries some depth owing to the specialized ageing process for the VDN.

60 ml (2 oz.) Rivesaltes Ambré, chilled
60 ml (2 oz.) tonic, chilled – plain or orange-flavoured

Pour Rivesaltes Ambré into bottom of a tall glass. Add chilled tonic. Add ice cubes to fill glass. Stir briefly before serving.

Le Soleil Catalan/Catalan Sun

60 ml (2 oz.) Rivesaltes Ambré
10 ml (⅓ oz.) Mirabelle (plum) syrup
20 ml (⅔ oz.) Nougatine liqueur
45 ml (1½ oz.) citrus-flavoured tonic
3 drops fresh lemon juice
nougat, fresh ground cherries, lime zest

Add all ingredients except tonic and garnishes to a shaker filled with ice and shake well. Strain into tall, chilled glass with ice. Top with tonic. Garnish with small squares of nougat, alternating with ground cherry halves on a short skewer, arranging a thin spiral of lime zest on top. Serve with a straw.

Maury Manhattan

This is like a Manhattan with vin doux naturel instead of sweet vermouth, says creator Jeff Harding. Harding honed his craft at New York's Waverly Inn, after working at numerous other establishments in New York, Miami and the Loire Valley of France.

60 ml (2 oz.) rye whiskey – preferably local Fort Hamilton if
you're in New York, otherwise Dickel's is great
30 ml (1 oz.) young red VDN such as Mas Amiel's Vintage Reserve
Maury or Coume du Roy Maury
1 brandied cherry

Stir over ice and strain into a Martini glass or Champagne coupe. Add brandied cherry to meld flavours.

Glossary

ageing
The stage of winemaking after fermentation. This can take place in any type and size of vessel. Different fortified wines have their own specific vessels, as well as amounts of time, locations and temperatures best suited to each one. Some sherries undergo 'biologic ageing', which takes place with a layer of flor (a type of yeast) on top of the surface of the wine.

angel's share
The liquid that evaporates from barrels while a wine or spirit is ageing, usually 3–6 per cent per year.

aromatized
A wine with specific herbs and spices added to enhance the aromas of the finished product.

artemisia, wormwood, *Wermut*
The herb that creates a defining characteristic of vermouth, especially in Italy, France and Spain. This herb is native to many mountainous areas in Europe. Different types of artemisia produce different effects. This herb must be used judiciously due to the active ingredient thujone, which can be present only in limited quantities in the finished wine.

base wine
Wine before it has any additives such as herbs, spices or distilled spirit.

bianco, blanc, blanco, white
Different wines have their own language norms for their 'white' versions. Here the word is listed in Italian, French, Spanish and English.

bitter, bitterness, bitters
Bitter and bitterness are sensory descriptions. However, bitters is a category of wine and/or spirits made with specialized, strong flavours and aromas; it is added by the drop to cocktails or other drinks.

bonbon
A large, round glass container containing many litres of wine. This word is specific to Roussillon. In other areas it is referred to as a demijohn.

brandy, unaged
The distilled spirit that is added to fortified wines, usually made with grapes in the case of fortified wines.

cinchona
A herb (bark) that is specific to vermouth, contributing bitterness in flavour as well as some reddish colour to the finished product. Quinine is also extracted from this bark.

digestif, digestivo
A style of wine or herbal spirit taken after dinner and believed to assist in digestion.

distillation, distilling
The process of creating the alcoholic spirit that is added to a wine to fortify it.

dry/extra dry/sweet
A descriptor that is specific to certain fortified wines, and indicates a relative dryness or sweetness of flavour, not an absolute value across categories. Most often, these words are used on a label in English, even in non-English speaking countries.

fortification
The addition of a distilled spirit to wine.

nero, noir, rojo, rosso, rouge, rubino
In English, some wine grapes are called 'red' grapes; in other languages these same grapes may be referred to as 'black' grapes (*nero* or *noir*). In a separate category, some finished, fortified wines such vermouth and Marsala may be termed 'red' (*rojo, rosso, rouge* or *rubino*) in the language native to the country where they are produced, regardless of the colour of the grapes used.

neutral (grapes, oak, spirit)
A term that refers to an ingredient or process that does not contribute strong flavours, aromas or colour to a finished wine.

mixology
A postmodern term for the act of mixing and/or developing new cocktails; creative bartenders are sometimes referred to as mixologists.

organoleptic
The sensory characteristics, primarily aromatics and flavours, in wine and spirits that make it possible for experienced tasters to accurately evaluate finished wines for their typicity.

solera
The process, characteristic of sherry production, also called fractional blending. A solera process is created when wine is removed for bottling from one or more barrels of wine, and then these barrels are topped up with younger wine from barrels stacked up above. On rare occasions, the solera system is used in the production of non-sherry wines.

spirit, spirits
Unaged distillates (or brandies) that are added to wines to fortify them.

Vitis vinifera
The genus and species of traditional wine grapes, which are of European/Asian origin.

Bibliography

Selected Publications

Daskal, Victoria, 'Massandra's Evolution', *The World of Fine Wine*,
    13 April 2018

Farrell, Joseph, *Sicily: A Cultural History* (Northampton, MA, 2014)

Giresse, Pierre, *Promenades géologiques en pays Catalan* (Canet, 2017)

González Gordon, Manuel M., *Sherry: the Noble Wine* (London, 1972)

Haine, W. Scott, *The History of France* (Westport, CT, 2000)

Hancock, David, *Oceans of Wine* (New Haven, CT, 2009)

Heckle, Harold, *A Traveller's Wine Guide to Spain* (Northampton, MA,
    2012)

Howkins, Ben, *Real Men Drink Port . . . and Ladies Do Too* (Shrewsbury,
    2011)

—, *Rich, Rare and Red: A Guide to Port* (Shrewsbury, 2014)

Jeffs, Julian, *Sherry* (Oxford, 2016)

Liddell, Alex, *Madeira: The Mid-Atlantic Wine* (London, 2014)

Liem, Peter, and Jésus Barquín, *Sherry, Manzanilla and Montilla:*
    A Guide to the Traditional Wines of Andalucía (New York, 2012)

Mayson, Richard, *Madeira: The Islands and Their Wines* (Oxford, 2016)

Norwich, John Julius, *Sicily: An Island at the Crossroads of History*
    (New York, 2015)

Piccinino, Fulvio, *Futurist Mixology* (Cocconato, 2016)

Port, Jeni, 'Apera, Anyone?', *Sydney Morning Herald*, www.smh.com.au, 22 May 2012

Robinson, Jancis, ed., *The Oxford Companion to Wine*, 4th edn (Oxford, 2015)

—, 'Massandra: Crimea's Liquid Crown Jewels', www.jancisrobinson.com, 14 April 2018

Saldana Sanchez, Cesar, *The Big Book of Sherry Wines* (Jerez, 2006)

Sedacca, Matthew, 'Why You Visit Madrid and Drink All the Vermouth', www.liquor.com, 10 August 2017

Simpson, James, *Creating Wine: The Emergence of a World Industry, 1840–1914* (Princeton, NJ, 2011)

Stewart, David, *Assimilation and Acculturation in Seventeenth-century Europe: Roussillon and France, 1659–1715* (Westport, CT, 1997)

Thach, Liz, 'Seasonal Sherry: The Extreme "Natural" Wine', www.winebusiness.com, 5 June 2018

Vrontis, Demetris, and Alkis Thrassou, 'The Renaissance of Commandaria: A Strategic Branding Prescriptive Analysis', *Journal for Global Business Advancement*, IV/4 (2011)

Websites

Achaia Clauss
www.achaiaclauss.gr

Berry Brothers & Rudd
www.bbr.com

Croft Port
www.croftport.com

Medarus
http://medarus.org

New Wines of Greece
www.newwinesofgreece.com

Port Cocktails
www.portcocktails.com

Rhone Wines
www.rhone-wines.com

Roussillon Wines
www.roussillon-wines.com

Tales of the Cocktail
https://talesofthecocktail.org

Vinho Madeira
www.vinhomadeira.pt

Vino Malaga
https://vinomalaga.com

Wines from Spain USA
https://winesfromspainusa.com

Acknowledgements

Vermouth

Eric Seed; Camper English; Roberto Bava and all the members of the Vermouth di Torino institute, especially the people at Del Professore, Carpano, Chazalettes, Cinzano, Giulio Cocchi, Drapò, Gancia, La Canellese, Martini & Rossi, and Tosti; Pierre-Olivier Rousseaux of Dolin; the people of Noilly Prat; Flore Mollard at Routin; Ellen Wallace and Nick Bates; Joan Tàpias and the Museu del Vermut.

Port

Adrian Bridge and Nick Heath of The Fladgate Partnership; Amanda Hathaway and the people at Wagstaff Worldwide; Andy Seymour of Beverage Alcohol Resource; Krista Drew of Pernod Ricard; George Sandeman and everyone at Sandeman; the Symington Family and everyone at Symington Family Estates; Ben Howkins; the IVDP, the Port and Douro Wines Institute.

Sherry

Cesar Saldana; Virginia Miller of Sherry Explorers; the people at Lustau, Gonzáles Byass and the Vinoble Wine Fair.

Madeira

Nadia Meroni; Gorete and everyone at IVBAM, the Madeira Wine, Embroidery and Handicraft Institute of Madeira; Bartholomew Broadbent; Juan Teixera, Julio Flores and everyone at Justino's; Joe and Lisa Saraiva and the volunteers at New Bedford's Feast of the Blessed Sacrament; Humberto Jadim and the people of Henriques & Henriques; the people of Blandy's, Madeira Wine Company, Barbeito, H. M. Borges and Madeira Vintners; Luis A. C. d'Oliveira of Pereira d'Oliveira.

Marsala

Christine Austin; Alessio Planeta and the people of Planeta; Marta Cilibrasi and everyone at Sopexa; Francesco Spadafora and his assistant Leonardo; the people at Tasca d'Almerita, Florio, Marco De Bartoli, Ciacco Putia Gourmet and Hotel Carmine; Maurizio Broggi, Education Director – Italian Wine Scholar, Wine Scholar Guild.

Vin Doux Naturel

Eric Aracil, Hélène Losada and everyone in Roussillon at the CIVR, Conseil Interprofessionnel des Vins du Roussillon; the people at Arnaud de Villaneuve, Mas Amiel, l'Etoile in Banyuls, Coume del Mas, Dom Brial, Jonquères d'Oriola, Terrassous, Domaine Treloar, Mas Becha and all the VDN producers of Roussillon; Jeff Harding of The Waverly Inn, New York; Stephanie Teuwen and the people at Inter-Rhone/VDN Rasteau.

And thanks for the general support by Branko Gerovac; Michael Lazar; Andy and Laurel Quady; Pirka Donini; Elisabetta Tosi; Mike Neebe; Maryna Calow at Wines of South Africa; Wine Australia; Alex Bridgeman of the Big Fortified Tasting; Jan Solomon; Ken Simonson.

Photo Acknowledgements

The author and publishers wish to express their thanks to the below sources of illustrative material and / or permission to reproduce it.

Photos by the author (Becky Sue Epstein): pp. 237, 238; courtesy the author: pp. 23, 45, 141 (top left), 141 (foot), 148, 165, 172, 176, 177 (foot), 180, 184 (foot), 200, 201; by permission from the author: pp. 204, 208 (foot), 212 (top), 216 (right), 221 (lower left), 225; © S. Ballard (2019): pp. 6–7, 19, 86, 95, 139, 179, 222; photo Basel University Library: p. 137; by kind permission of the Conseil Interprofessionnel des Vins du Roussillon (CIVR): pp. 208 (top), 212 (foot), 216 (left), 217, 221 (top and lower right); used by kind permission of Consejo Regulador Jerez: pp. 96, 97, 101, 105, 109, 120; photo Conudrum: p. 240 (foot); photos Branko Gerovac: pp. 33, 37, 40, 41, 116; photos reproduced by kind permission of Giulio Cocchi Spumanti Srl: pp. 12, 28, 34, 36; photo LEBAETOAL: p. 65; photo Library of Congress, Washington, DC (Prints and Photographs Division): p. 20; used by kind permission of the Madeira Wine Company: p. 149; courtesy of Madeira Wine Institute: p. 161; photo Martini & Rossi NYC: p. 49; photos used by kind permission of Symington Family Estates: pp. 56, 68, 69, 88; photos used with the kind permission of Taylor's Port: pp. 59, 62, 63, 64, 74, 85; photos Juan Teixeira, reproduced by kind permission: p. 141 (top right), 153, 156, 168; © 2016 Liz

Index